SPEAK

WITH

CONFIDENCE

SPEAK

WITH

CONFIDENCE

Overcome Self-Doubt, Communicate Clearly, and Inspire Your Audience

MIKE ACKER

WILEY

Published by John Wiley & Sons, Inc., Hoboken, New Jersey.
Published simultaneously in Canada.

No part of this publication may be reproduced, stored in a retrieval system, or transmitted in any form or by any means, electronic, mechanical, photocopying, recording, scanning, or otherwise, except as permitted under Section 107 or 108 of the 1976 United States Copyright Act, without either the prior written permission of the Publisher, or authorization through payment of the appropriate per-copy fee to the Copyright Clearance Center, Inc., 222 Rosewood Drive, Danvers, MA 01923, (978) 750-8400, fax (978) 750-4470, or on the web at www.copyright.com. Requests to the Publisher for permission should be addressed to the Permissions Department, John Wiley & Sons, Inc., 111 River Street, Hoboken, NJ 07030, (201) 748-6011, fax (201) 748-6008, or online at http://www.wiley.com/go/permission.

Trademarks: Wiley and the Wiley logo are trademarks or registered trademarks of John Wiley & Sons, Inc. and/or its affiliates in the United States and other countries and may not be used without written permission. All other trademarks are the property of their respective owners. John Wiley & Sons, Inc. is not associated with any product or vendor mentioned in this book.

Limit of Liability/Disclaimer of Warranty: While the publisher and author have used their best efforts in preparing this book, they make no representations or warranties with respect to the accuracy or completeness of the contents of this book and specifically disclaim any implied warranties of merchantability or fitness for a particular purpose. No warranty may be created or extended by sales representatives or written sales materials. The advice and strategies contained herein may not be suitable for your situation. You should consult with a professional where appropriate. Further, readers should be aware that websites listed in this work may have changed or disappeared between when this work was written and when it is read. Neither the publisher nor authors shall be liable for any loss of profit or any other commercial damages, including but not limited to special, incidental, consequential, or other damages.

For general information on our other products and services or for technical support, please contact our Customer Care Department within the United States at (800) 762-2974, outside the United States at (317) 572-3993 or fax (317) 572-4002.

Wiley also publishes its books in a variety of electronic formats. Some content that appears in print may not be available in electronic formats. For more information about Wiley products, visit our web site at www.wiley.com.

Library of Congress Cataloging-in-Publication Data:

Names: Acker, Mike, author.
Title: Speak with confidence : overcome self-doubt, communicate clearly,
   and inspire your audience / Mike Acker.
Description: Hoboken, New Jersey : John Wiley & Sons, Inc., 2022. |
   Includes index.
Identifiers: LCCN 2022032870 (print) | LCCN 2022032871 (ebook) | ISBN
   9781394159741 (cloth) | ISBN 9781394159765 (ePub) | ISBN 9781394159772
   (ePDF)
Subjects: LCSH: Public speaking. | Public speaking—Psychological aspects.
Classification: LCC PN4129.15 .A28 2023 (print) | LCC PN4129.15 (ebook) |
   DDC 808.5/1—dc23/eng/20220715
LC record available at https://lccn.loc.gov/2022032870
LC ebook record available at https://lccn.loc.gov/2022032871

Cover Design: Paul McCarthy

SKY10037197_102122

CONTENTS

READ FIRST

Thank you for investing in my book.

As an appreciation, I'd love to give you a free gift.

> The "3 & 3" Video Course

This course covers the "3 Classics" that are the basis of effective public speaking and the "3 Questions" that will help you write better speeches.

It's the foundation of my coaching and has helped hundreds of people gain clarity and direction in creating their speech.

Visit this link or use the QR code for your free gift: https://content.mikeacker.com

INTRODUCTION
The Framework for Confidence

I just bought my first sailboat . . .

For $1,000, and I quickly realized it was going to be the most expensive $1,000 I'd ever spent. This realization led me to sell the boat one month after my acquisition. Having never owned a boat before, I learned a lot in that month about remodeling, sailing techniques, and the many names of ropes. I also learned that boats are a great analogy for *confidence*.

Imagine a three-masted schooner braving high winds and floating chunks of ice to bring life-saving medicine to a town on the far side of Lake Superior. Or Norwegian explorer Thor Heyerdahl and his crew sailing across the Pacific in an unpowered handmade raft to demonstrate that the Polynesian Islands could have been populated by South Americans. Or a crew of crabbers returning from frigid Alaskan waters, loaded down with their precious cargo. Or a state of the art, carbon fiber trimaran tacking back and forth against the wind, an expert crew sailing her at seemingly impossible speeds in hopes of the America's Cup.

Or a canoe piloted by a drunken thrill-seeker heading toward Niagara Falls.

To many people, the idea of public speaking is as frightening as heading over Niagara in a canoe. But I want you to imagine a world without inspiring speeches such as Martin Luther King, Jr.'s "I Have a Dream" or Patrick Henry's "Give Me Liberty or

Give Me Death." For as long as humans have been talking, there have been those brave enough to risk rejection and speak out to lead and influence others.

In my top-rated book *Speak with No Fear*, I say that public speaking is a "universal advantage"—a skill that gives you a leg up in nearly any profession or situation. That book's popularity demonstrated how many people face paralyzing fear at the thought of giving a speech or presentation. To follow the boating analogy, that book was written for those who suffered from aquaphobia, with the goal of getting them off the dock and into the boat—without throwing up.

My assumption is that you come to this book with at least a little speaking experience and don't suffer from debilitating fear. Otherwise, I'd encourage you to put this book on pause and read *Speak with No Fear* first. Fear is a very powerful emotion and can literally hijack your ability to learn, but that book teaches you how to convert paralyzing fear into power.

Bonus: Download the *Speak with No Fear Action Checklist* for free at https://swnf2.mikeacker.com

This book is the next step. I don't want to just get you into the boat; I want to teach you to confidently sail to your desired destination. The goal isn't merely surviving but *thriving*.

The single greatest requirement for great speaking is . . . confidence. Not a deep, authoritative voice or TED Talk–worthy material. Confidence. I have a friend who went to Honduras on a mission trip with only one year of Spanish—from a teacher who didn't really speak it—while some of his teammates had taken three or more years. But he ended up speaking more Spanish than any of them. Why? Because he had the confidence to try, fail, and try again.

The single greatest skill required for great speaking is confidence.

Said another way, it doesn't matter how nice your boat is; it's useless if you don't have the confidence to push away from the dock.

Think about what "confidence" means. It comes from the Latin, *fidere*, "to trust" and *con*, an intensifying prefix. So, confidence means a full and complete trust, belief in the ability or trustworthiness of a person or thing. Belief in oneself.

But simply believing in yourself doesn't mean anything. Countless cringe-worthy performers on *American Idol* and *America's Got Talent* believed in themselves. The drunken thrill-seeker in the canoe has confidence. Confidence must be grounded in reality. It is only as good as the abilities behind it.

Confidence is only as good as the abilities behind it.

Confidence is also a two-way street. Not only must you have faith in yourself and your abilities, but your audience must also have faith in you or else they won't listen. You literally have seconds from the time you reach the lectern or get introduced in a Zoom meeting to when they decide whether or not they'll trust you with their time and attention.

That is to say, this book isn't a "just believe in yourself" collection of inspirational quotes. It is a proven pathway to becoming a capable and confident speaker who makes an impact.

This book is a proven pathway to becoming a capable and confident speaker that makes an impact.

I've spent over two decades developing this pathway, studying communication from every angle, speaking to crowds of every size, and coaching speakers of every background: a UFC heavyweight champion, politicians, CEOs of multibillion-dollar companies, but also to students, engineers, ESL speakers, and professionals at all levels. People just like you. What I'm saying is I've seen this framework work.

This is my sixth book about communication, but it was supposed to be my first. When I started writing it, I thought, *Not yet, Mike. You have more to learn and process*. I knew it was too important a topic to rush. Now, I'm ready, and I'm excited about everything I have to teach.

Confidence on stage follows you off stage.

I went to a fairly small private university with a debate team that held its own against far more prominent schools. Year after year, Professor Gary Gillespie led Northwest University to win at national and international tournaments. In *Speak with No Fear*, I talk about how Gillespie first talked me into joining the team in spite of my self-doubt and then believed in me until I learned to believe in myself.

Gillespie taught us more than debate tricks. Using Aristotle's famous three elements of persuasion—*ethos, pathos*, and *logos*—he taught us that communication was bigger than technique and the words we used. It flowed from who we are as people.

I said earlier that confidence is the single most important skill required for great speaking. Let me add to that a little. Confidence is one of the greatest skills for *life*. When you learn to communicate with confidence, it bleeds over into every area. Because my framework is holistic—addressing the entire person and not just the exterior skills—your confidence on stage will follow you off stage.

Bonus: Download a quick *Confidence Cheatsheet* for free at
https://cheatsheet.mikeacker.com

For many people, their three biggest concerns are their health, wealth, and relationships. Confidence has a positive impact on all three.

1. *Health*: Excessive stress is one of the greatest threats to well-being. Not only will confidence lower your "pre-speech jitters"—the sleepless nights, anxiety, and racing heart—but will also help you face your off-stage stresses with calm.

2. *Wealth*: As I said, confident public speaking skills will increase your value to your organization, no matter your profession. And as your confidence bleeds into the rest of your professional life, you will interview better, sell better, and lead better. I've had several clients get promoted midway through our work together or find the courage to apply for positions that they previously dismissed as "out of their league."

3. *Relationship*: Health and wealth mean nothing if you are relationally miserable—if you're lonely and too timid to invite a colleague to have lunch or ask someone out on a date or if you're too scared to deal with an issue that is slowly driving you and your spouse apart. My book *Connect Through Emotional Intelligence* deals with this at a deeper level, but confidence is key to healthy relationships. (Conversely, improving your emotional intelligence will help your confidence become well grounded—I think every "*American Idol* fail" could have been avoided with a higher E.I.)

Confidence is a key to healthy relationships.

So, are you ready to begin your journey to speaking—and living—with confidence? You will learn these things like:

- Systems for nailing off-the-cuff speeches.

- Combating "imposter syndrome."

- Finding your greatness and how to stop comparing yourself to others.

- Adding interest to your verbal delivery.

I'm not promising an easy path. This will take work. You have to be willing to do more and push harder than others. But it will be worth it. I am *confident* that the payoff will far exceed your investment.

Don't let insecurities hijack another speech or ruin another opportunity. Gain the confidence that will transform your life.

CHAPTER 1

The Big Three

My coaching career started as a side hustle. Ever since college, I'd been working with professionals to improve their leadership and communication. My role as an executive director of a nonprofit involved training my team, and I take pride in how many of them have gone on to new heights. My personal mission was and, still is, to help people realize their potential.

In my thirties, I had a career change and was finding success in consultative sales. I enjoyed my work but missed the mentoring aspect and kept finding chances to work with leaders and speakers on the side. I didn't initially think of it as a side hustle. It was more of a paid hobby.

Then I got my first big deal coaching opportunity. The CEO of a nationally known marketing firm learned about me from a referral and reached out, but she wanted more than feedback and informal coaching. She was looking for an A-to-Z program. So, I consolidated everything I'd learned and taught into a comprehensive system. Reaching back to my time with Professor Gillespie, I started by walking her through Aristotle's elements of persuasion.

1. Ethos

Speakers need to convince the listener of their credibility (*ethos* is the root of ethical). The audience needs to feel like they can trust, learn from, and connect to you. You must build rapport through relevant stories, the words you use, the way you conform to the context of the event, and your connection to your message. When the audience trusts and connects with the speaker, they listen with greater receptivity.

> **When the audience trusts and connects with the speaker, they listen with greater receptivity.**

2. Pathos

This means to evoke emotions. Your message must affect *you* before it can possibly affect your audience. Then you must intentionally use stories, evocative analogies, and emotional tone to convey the meaning behind the message. True communication is more than the mere transference of knowledge. When you feel your message, your audience will feel it with you.

> **When you feel your message, your audience will feel it with you.**

3. Logos

Logos encompasses organization and thought and creating understanding. It is the *logic* of the message. You must utilize various tools to persuade the audience: case studies, facts, citations, research, statistics, and recognized authorities. These types of proofs make your material more persuasive and help you win the audience over. You must have something worth saying and do the work of framing it in a way that appeals to the head.

I went on to tell this CEO that effective communication requires all three. Too many speakers fail to establish a connection through *ethos* or engage feelings through *pathos*, relying on *logos* alone. But your audience is not comprised of soulless androids. They are emotional beings and rely on intuition as much as intellect. If you want to impact your listeners, you must use all three elements of persuasion.

We are emotional beings and rely on intuition as much as intellect.

After I'd gone through all this with the CEO, her response forced me to reevaluate my brand-new coaching curriculum.

"Mike, that's good stuff, but it's useless to me. I'm too nervous to even get up on stage, let alone think about elements of persuasion."

Useless? Shoot. Now what?

I had to peel back all my memories, back to when I was a frightened seventh grader in Mexico who gave himself a psychosomatic fever to avoid speaking in front of the class and to remember how I evolved to become a confident speaker. Over nearly twenty years of experience and education, I had intuitively developed my own three "sources of confidence." Once I systematized those, I was able to help that CEO. This formed the foundation for my programs, communication workshops, and now this book.

This proved so effective that I began receiving more and more referrals. Even as I kept the sales job, my "hobby" became a registered business, and I had to hire staff. I was coaching, speaking, and giving workshops; something had to give, and I made the leap of faith into full-time coaching, speaking, and writing—and I'm loving it!

THE SOURCES OF CONFIDENCE

I want you to think back to the last time you heard a speech that moved you. Maybe it was a politician that made you believe in a better future. Maybe it was a motivational speaker that inspired you to push yourself further. Or maybe it was a coworker who made you think, *I wish I could speak like that!*

Speakers like that are marked by genuine confidence. Not hold-my-beer-and-watch-this confidence, but confidence that holds the speaker steady and inspires the audience. Confidence like that isn't a single thing but a combination of your identity, your message, and your skills.

True confidence is found where these three circles meet—when you have determined your identity, defined your message, and developed your skills. In this chapter, I will walk you through the 10,000-foot view of each and what happens when any one of them is lacking. From there, I'll devote a section to mastering each component.

1. Determine Your Identity

I began this book by asking you to imagine a schooner, a handmade raft, and other boats. Your identity—the collection of your strengths and weaknesses, experiences, personality, and deep-seated values—is like one of those boats. Each one is different and is meant for different kinds of tasks. At the same time, boats can be modified within certain limits. Confidence comes from knowing your boat, what it is capable of, what kind of shape it is in, and where you can improve it.

I'll frequently have prospective clients ask, "Mike, can you teach me some new techniques and skills, so I can feel more confident?"

My response? "Yes, but let's start with laying the foundation before jumping to the finishing touches."

I'm not doing them any good by showing how to run up the mainsail if their boat is taking on water by the gallon. Before we address your message or add new skills, you need to do the deep work of determining who you are.

Notice that I said *determine* your identity, not *discover*. There is a discovery element to it, but it doesn't stop there. One of my favorite sayings is "Where you are isn't where you have to stay." There are parts of your identity that you need to accept, but there are others you can improve.

Where you are isn't where you have to stay.

In the first section of this book, I will walk you through understanding and determining your identity. By the time you finish that section, you will have a clear idea of who you are as a speaker, how the message flows from you, and which parts of yourself you need to embrace, accept, or improve.

2. Define Your Message

The movie *Dunkirk* tells the real-life story of the mass evacuation of British forces out of France at the beginning of World War II. With German forces speeding toward Dunkirk, the call went out across England for all available boats to sail the Channel and save as many soldiers as possible. The response was overwhelming as everything from luxury yachts to barely-more-than-lifeboats braved the German Luftwaffe and made the dangerous trip. Countless professional and amateur sailors risked their lives because they understood that their "cargo" was precious.

If you and your identity are the boat, your message is the cargo. Would you risk your life and reputation to deliver a boat-load of plastic trinkets? Probably not. But to save your fellow citizens from the Nazi war machine? I'd like to think I would've sailed my $1,000 boat to Dunkirk for that.

What if your "cargo" feels like plastic trinkets? Many of my clients struggle because *they're* bored by their topic—routine updates, IT protocols, sales trends and graphs, key performance indicators (KPIs), and returns on investment (ROIs). But part of confidence in your message comes from connecting to its deeper meaning and purpose. If it's worth saying, then it's worth caring about. Every business is ultimately about people, and people are worth our emotional investment. But I'm getting ahead of myself.

If it's worth saying, then it's worth caring about.

In the second section, we'll begin by digging into your message and what it means to your audience. Then I'll teach you how to efficiently craft and effectively deliver it. This will cover not only prepared speeches but also off-the-cuff presentations and meetings. By the time you finish that section, you'll gain the confidence to speak in any situation.

3. Develop Skills

Have you ever watched someone who excel in their craft? It almost doesn't matter what they're doing—glassblowing, playing guitar, bartending, handling a sailboat—there is an artistry to how their hands seem to move of their own accord. I recently listened to leadership expert John Maxwell speak. That man's been speaking longer than I've been alive. He employed all the skills and techniques that I teach but so seamlessly that I didn't even notice. I just knew I was in the hands of a master.

If your identity is the boat and your message the cargo, then your skills are your *speaking* skills. Pretty straightforward there.

In the third section, we'll cover a host of tricks and techniques that are so practical that you might be tempted to skip ahead. Don't do it. I intentionally placed skills last because they are built upon the foundation of identity and message. By the time you finish that section, you will have a box full of tools that you know how to use.

HEART, HEAD, AND HAND

Identity, message, and skills—all three are vital. Another way I like to describe it is:

- Identity is your heart—*who* is saying it.
- Message is your head—*what* is being said.
- Skills are your hands—*how* it is being said.

Confident speaking—speaking that flows from your confidence and makes an impact on the listener—requires all three components working in conjunction.

What happens if one is missing?

If someone has identity and message but lack the skills, they are **boring**. You can probably name a few seasoned professors who really knew their stuff but put you to sleep. For the Harry Potter fans out there, this is Professor Binns, teacher of History of Magic, who could make the goblin rebellion boring.

If someone has identity and skills but lacks a message, they are simply **entertainers**. People enjoy listening to them but leave unchanged. There's nothing wrong with that if your goal is entertainment, but I believe you want more for your audience. You want them to think, feel, or do something new because of you. These speakers are like Professor Trelawney, the divination teacher. She put on quite a show for her believers, but there's no meaning behind almost any of her predictions (and I don't think she gets any credit for her two real prophecies).

Finally, if someone has a message and skills but no identity, they (at best) have no depth. At worst, they are **hypocrites**. They look great on stage, but it falls apart when you get up close. These are like Gilderoy Lockhart. Big talk, lots of style, but it's all fake. Let's be honest: These are the most dangerous of the three. Many of us grew up listening to Bill Cosby, laughing at his jokes and wishing our dads were as wise and cool as Cliff Huxtable. When the reality of his character came out, we were left stunned and heartbroken.

At this moment, who do you feel the most like: Binns, Trelawney, or Lockhart? Or do you feel any of those would be a step up for you because you lack identity, message, *and* skills?

Then you are in the right place.

Over the rest of this book, I'll apply this framework to your speaking, so you can be like—who else?—Albus Dumbledore. Confidence and influence flows from speakers who have identity, message, and skills.

Confidence and influence flows from speakers who have identity, message, and skills.

PROVEN PATHS TO (FALSE) CONFIDENCE

Before we get started, it's vital to understand that confidence is not an absence of fear. In proper doses, fear is a tonic. Every speech should stir up some level of nervousness within you—it does me! In *Speak with No Fear*, I spend an entire chapter on channeling those nerves into energy and emotion (i.e. *pathos*).

No one enjoys fear, but attempting to eliminate it altogether will take you down one of the two proven paths to *false* confidence. Those paths are arrogance and apathy. Either of them will ensure feelings of confidence but at the cost of effectiveness and connection.

Arrogance says, "I don't need this book. My audience is lucky to have me." It takes over when we impress ourselves—perhaps because we're subconsciously afraid we don't measure up.

Apathy says, "It's not worth the effort to read this book. My audience is going to show up anyway because they have to." It creeps in when we no longer care and are too lazy to change.

Arrogant speakers are often seen among politicians, rising stars, and even in churches. Apathetic speakers fill long-time management positions, academia, and sectors that don't require them to prioritize quality in communication.

The fact you've read this far tells me that neither apathy nor arrogance have taken over—yet. But they are constant temptations to every speaker (and leader). In Chapter 3, we'll talk more about them, and how they're common reactions to personal shortcomings.

Apathy and arrogance are constant temptations to every speaker.

All this is to say that as you go on this journey toward confidence, be on the lookout for creeping arrogance ("I don't need this!") and apathy ("Who really cares?"). Pay particular attention to *when* they try to creep in. Don't be surprised if it's when I touch a nerve. As we'll see in the next section, true confidence goes far deeper than your ability to give a presentation, and we'll end up touching on things like self-worth, emotional intelligence, and your personal values.

Will it be hard work? Absolutely. But the payoff will extend far beyond a single speech.

PART I

DETERMINE YOUR IDENTITY

CHAPTER 2

You Are the Message

Y̲ou are the message.

If all your company needed was information, then they could cancel the presentation and play the slide deck. If all they needed was statistics, an email would be sufficient. You, in your own personhood, bring an irreplaceable element to the presentation.

You are the message.

For example, I've been speaking professionally for almost twenty years and have taken more classes than you can imagine, and have read more books than you can count. Am I perfect? By no means. But I do know what I'm talking about. When I speak about speaking, it comes from inside of me. It is part of who I am. Contrast that with a politician reading a speech that someone else wrote, about an issue he doesn't understand, to people he has no connection with.

When you are asked to give a presentation, relay a report, or speak to your team, it means they need *you*—not your slideshow or handouts. When I first started writing, I was reluctant to share all my insights for fear of undercutting my coaching business, but I discovered that people are *more* likely to hire me if I "give away" everything. They understand that the message I have in me is bigger than what's on the page and that's worth paying for.

They need you—not your slideshow or handouts.

Going back to Aristotle, PowerPoint obviously cannot provide the *ethos* and *pathos*. And it can't provide all the *logos* either. This is something *you* know about. These ideas are something you have a vested interest in. Your speech carries part of you. If anyone else were to give the same presentation, it would not be the same.

So, you are the message. You are the boat that carries the cargo. Without you, the real message won't ever arrive at its destination. For that reason, your identity is foundational to confidence.

SETTING THE FOUNDATION

If you've read any of my other books, then you may already know a little about my story. My mother was a witch (literally), and my father was a drug smuggler, which is how he learned to speak Spanish and fly (literally and figuratively). Before I was born, they began to turn their lives around, and then several years later when I was ten, they founded an NGO in Mazatlán, Mexico.

Moving to Mexico as a scrawny white kid and living there until college is part of who I am. I understand different cultures more easily than most, am fluent in Spanish, and know what it feels like to be an outsider. My parents' love for Mazatlán is also part of who I am. As an adult, I've led many groups there to build houses for those in need. The first part of the process was always to pour the foundation and wait four days for it to set.

It drove me crazy. *Come on!* I'd think. *Let's get going.* I was in a hurry to get to the real work of putting up walls and running wire. (We'll get back to that impatience in just a moment.) But experienced builders understand that without a strong foundation, everything else is a waste. One hard rain (and it could really rain in Mazatlán) and all would be lost.

In this chapter, we aren't going to work on the act of speaking as much as the foundation of who you are as a speaker and person. Without that foundation, you can create a great message and present it with great skill only to collapse under the pressure of a single criticism (does that sound familiar?). But with it, you're more than halfway to dealing with your nervousness, insecurity, and imposter syndrome.

TO THINE OWN SELF BE TRUE

Shakespeare was the second-greatest source of English expressions (the first was the King James Bible). From him we got, "it's Greek to me," "pound of flesh," "dead as a doornail," and more. Polonius's speech in *Hamlet* has several memorable quotes, but best known is:

> *This above all: to thine own self be true,*
> *And it must follow, as the night the day,*
> *Thou canst not then be false to any man.*

Your identity as a speaker must be built upon who you really are—and not you acting like someone else or trying to be what others want (or what you *think* they want). Otherwise, you will be false to every man and woman.

Oxford Languages defines identity as "the fact of being who a person is." That's *really* helpful . . . Identity remains a vague subject. Psychologists, philosophers, and theologians wrestle with what it means to be "me." It remains of intense interest for academia and pop culture, but I'm neither a psychologist nor a philosopher. I'm an executive and communication coach. This section won't delve into existentialism, but it will be a practical approach to discovering and defining your self-image because how you perceive yourself drives how you *show* yourself.

How you perceive yourself drives how you show yourself.

So, what is your identity as a speaker? It is the combination of your personality, voice, beliefs, choices, responses, values, positions, perspectives, outlooks, successes, failures, fears, dreams, knowledge, and experiences—and how they play themselves out when you speak. This speaking identity encompasses self-image (how you perceive yourself when you speak), self-esteem (the value you place on yourself as you communicate), and self-hood (the uniqueness that you bring when you present).

How is this identity different from your regular, nonspeaker identity? Can't you just be like an actor who is one thing on stage and another off? Sure, but it's a really bad idea. Let me explain why.

PERSONHOOD OR PERSONA?

When I'm working with my clients, I draw a little stickman (I'm not a great artist, and I own that part of my identity):

This is your identity—how you see yourself. It's the most real, authentic version of you when you're around people you're really comfortable with. But then you get a promotion that feels a little beyond your natural abilities. Maybe you think you need to be more extroverted or sound more intelligent. So, you create a layer on top of the real you:

Then your boss asks you to give a presentation at the next meeting. Without realizing it, you immediately access a file of great speakers you've heard or admire and that you want to be like (and think you *should* be like). You begin telling yourself great speakers need to do XYZ even though you're more of an LMNO person. So, you put a layer of XYZ on top of the previous one:

I had one client, naturally enthusiastic and full of energy, who said, "I need to be calm, cool, and collected. Mike, you have to teach me to be calm, cool, and collected." Why? Because he thought that was more professional, but what made him invaluable to his team was his enthusiasm. Over the years, I've seen people become totally different people on stage—and that on stage persona was *always* a step down from their real-life personhood.

On stage persona is always a step down from real-life personhood.

I once worked with an Army officer who wanted to be more like an officer she knew when she'd first joined.

"What was he like?" I asked.

"Really big and tall," she said. "He had this booming voice. Really authoritative, you know? When he walked into a room, he just commanded attention."

That was not who my client was. As a petite woman of color, she had a completely different sense about herself. Very educated and incredibly sharp, she genuinely cared about her team and listened intently when they talked to her. She may not have commanded attention the moment she entered a room, but she had earned everyone's respect and the U.S. Army would've lost something if she'd taken on the persona she initially wanted.

Once you get into the habit of creating a persona, it gets more difficult to return to your true self when you speak. As you experience more success, the expectations increase, as does the feeling that the *real* you is inadequate, so you are forced to add more layers. On the outside, you may look the part, but on the inside, you'll feel like an imposter—hence the imposter syndrome (we'll talk about that in Chapter 5).

The farther and farther these outer layers of speaker-identity expand away from our true identity, the less recognizable we will be, even to ourselves. One episode of ESPN's *30 for 30*, which highlighted various athletes and sports stories, featured Brian Bosworth, better remembered by Seahawk fans (like me) as "The Boz." He was the highest-paid rookie in his day and was well-known for his arrogance and theatrics—including arriving for training in a helicopter. In an interview, a former teammate basically said, "Bosworth was actually a great guy, but The Boz was a jerk." Over time, the persona took over, and even Brian didn't like who he became.

Does this sound extreme? It all starts with the first layer, and as new challenges and opportunities that exceed your capacities arise, you are forced to add new layers. The persona begins to overshadow the personhood, and you forget who you really are— Brian or The Boz.

Are you starting to see why it's so important for your speaker-identity to match your authentic self? Here are four more reasons:

First, maintaining those layers is a lot of work. In *Speak with No Fear*, one of my strategies is "You Be You," and I compare identity to holding a big dictionary. If you hold it close to your chest, it will weigh nothing at all. But if you hold it out at arm's length, separate from yourself, those 20 to 40 pounds are going to get heavy fast. Acting a part requires a massive amount of mental and emotional energy that steals bandwidth from your message. Each new layer requires more energy, risking eventual collapse.

Second, people are more perceptive than you think. Sooner or later, they'll realize you're an actor. Only they'll call it being a fake. You'll lose your *ethos* and the audience with it.

Third, *you'll* know you're a fake—inviting the imposter syndrome—and that's more corrosive to confidence than gasoline to Styrofoam.

Being a fake is more corrosive to confidence than gasoline to Styrofoam.

Fourth, it's no fun because no one enjoys feeling like a fake. On a very deep level, always acting a part and never being yourself cause you to live in a continual state of dis-ease.

What's the solution? What do you do when your true identity is not equal to the tasks? In my coaching session, I click "undo," removing the layers one by one and replacing it with this:

Rather than adding exterior layers to your speaker identity, we want to grow the interior. That's our goal for the rest of this section. We'll begin by discovering who you are and giving you a paradigm for how to work on yourself. Then we'll look at how to actively determine your identity as a speaker. Remember, it's not just what you say or how you say it: You are the message. After that, we'll deal with some of the main challenges to your identity, including the imposter syndrome, victim mentality, comparisons, and how to deal with rejection. As I said, this book is called *Speak with Confidence*, but this confidence is going to spill out into the rest of your life.

CHAPTER 3

Determine and Discover

T ime for another great quote:

Γνωθι σευτον

Translation: "Know thyself." To the ancient Greek philosophers, knowing yourself was central to the meaning of life. It wasn't something found in a single self-help book but a lifetime of pursuit. The better you understand your identity, the better you can build upon that foundation for greater confidence in speaking. You will discover that *you* are a far better person than any persona you can create.

STRENGTHS DISGUISED AS WEAKNESSES

I've always struggled with impatience. Nothing happened fast enough, and I frequently found myself frustrated with everyone else's pace.

As a young executive director at a nonprofit in Washington State, I was seeing a lot of success in my work and wanted to expand to a second location. Something like that typically takes as much as a year to plan and execute. But I have a mantra that's behind much of my success (and failures): "If it's worth doing in the year, it's worth doing in a month."

I couldn't understand why my board—capable business leaders with years of combined experience—kept dragging their feet. Then I discovered the CliftonStrengths assessment (for-merly StrengthsFinder), which revealed my top five strengths and how best to utilize them.

At the top of my list: Activator. I don't talk about doing things; I make things happen. My impatience isn't a character flaw—it's part of my strength. Obviously, this isn't an excuse to be a jerk, and the more I understand what's behind my impa-tience, the easier it is for me to accommodate those who dif-fer from me.

This also helped me understand my board. They weren't being obstinate; they were working out of their strengths. This included thinking strategically, not just asking if we *could* do it but if we *should* do it. I've since learned how important it is to work with people whose strengths balance mine.

Another premise of CliftonStrengths was that we should work harder capitalizing on our strengths than improving our weaknesses. If your high schooler keeps coming home with A's in Math, but C's in Language Arts, your focus should be on the A's, not the C's. He's probably never going to be an amazing writer but shows real promise as an engineer. Lean into that. Likewise, I could work really hard on improving my artistic skills, but I'll never be a Van Gogh. Instead, I should (and did) devote all my energy to developing my leadership and commu-nication skills.

You are a complex mixture of strengths and weaknesses. "Know thyself" means discovering your strengths and building on them. It means acknowledging your weakness (more on that in a moment) and making accommodations for them. Do you have a good sense of your abilities? We'll talk more about how to handle your weaknesses soon, but can you list ten things you appreciate? Ten reasons why you enjoy being you? If not, I really recommend CliftonStrengths. I've known people whose lives were changed when they discovered what they did well.

IT'S ALL ABOUT PERSONALITY

Another popular tool is the Myers-Briggs Personality Assessment. It measures things like introversion and extroversion. Then there's also various assessments that measure "the big five" elements of personality: extraversion, neuroticism, agreeableness, conscientiousness, and openness to experience.

The DISC assessment looks at the four different styles of human behavior: dominance (D), influence (I), steadiness (S), and conscientiousness (C). What makes it unique is that it also looks at your *natural* versus *adaptive* tendencies, i.e. how you operate in normal situations and how you operate in stressful ones. Just as we saw above, you have a natural personhood (and speaking style) as well as an adaptive persona that you tend toward under pressure.

The Enneagram has become very popular in recent years and focuses on what motivates you. Helping people? Being right? Avoiding pain? Being an individual?

There are many personality assessments available online (of varying quality). If you haven't already, take several versions of the above. As you compare the results, don't ask if you *like* them but if you recognize yourself in them. The goal isn't entertainment like with a Facebook "Which *Friends* character are you?" quiz. Seriously, who cares about that stuff? Though, I'm a "Monica," in case you were wondering. The purpose of any assessment should be discovering the following:

- What strengths should you be building on?
- Which weaknesses should you accommodate?
- Which should you try to improve?

Think again of the different kinds of boats. If you are a slow but powerful tugboat, don't waste time trying to go faster. Learn how to use that power to move others. If you're a zippy little speed boat, learn how to use that speed. If you're a party boat, enjoy the fact that everyone wants to be around you.

I've worked with hundreds of speakers, and each one is different. My goal is never to press them into a TED Talk mold (and it definitely has a preferred mold) but help them discover what *they* can do better than anything else.

- Some speakers speak with gravitas, an old term suggesting depth and wisdom.

- Some speakers radiate infectious energy.

- Some speakers make a big crowd feel like a small family.

Discovering your true self is the first step to discovering your speaking identity. You will be at your best—and most confident—when your speaking style is aligned with your personality.

You will be at your best when your speaking style is aligned with your personality.

Maybe right now you're thinking something like, "What if I don't have any speaking strengths to build on?" I've coached a lot of people and have yet to find someone that doesn't have any. What I have found is people whose strengths need to be developed.

You Aren't Perfect

A lot of songs out there try to tell you that you're perfect. They're lying. You are worthy of love and acceptance just the way you are, but we have room for improvement. That's why you bought this book.

Every one of my clients comes to me because they want to get better, but there needs to be a happy balance between the things you appreciate about yourself, the things you try to improve, and the things you make accommodations for. How do you know which is which? After I draw my mediocre stickmen to describe my client's authentic self, I use the "Shapes" tool to make a graph with three perfect bars:

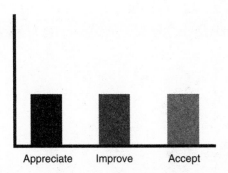

Appreciate Improve Accept

Appreciate: These are the things that you like about your-self, strengths that you know how to use to their greatest advantage. You enjoy them but aren't arrogant.

Improve: These are areas of deficiency. You know about them and are actively working on them.

Accept: These are the weaknesses you just need to accept and have found ways to accommodate.

As a silly example, back in the day, I really *appreciated* my glorious long, blond hair and have the photos to prove it. Then, when I realized I was beginning to lose my amazing hair, I worked to *improve* my image by keeping it short and bulking up my shoulders. Eventually, I'll need to *accept* it and follow in my dad's footsteps by shaving off the diminishing remains.

The graph goes from 0 to 100, and there are a total of 100 "points" are available for all three bars combined. If you're too high in one, the others automatically become lower. This is a key principle: Your goal is to keep all three roughly even because each of the three possible misalignments creates a specific type of confidence-destroyer. If someone is too high on appreciate, they'll become narcissistic. If someone is too high on improve, they'll experience imposter syndrome. If someone is too high on accept, they'll fall into a victim mentality. Let's dig into these misalignments.

1. High Appreciation Misalignment: Narcissism

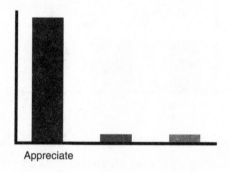

Appreciate

Appreciating everything about yourself is lower-case "n" narcissism. You think you're wonderful, refuse to acknowledge any weakness, and lose all opportunity for improvement. And since you refuse to acknowledge your weaknesses, you can't accept or make accommodations for them. Another consequence is that you tend not to have any deep relationships because relationships require honesty, and, honestly, nobody is "100% appreciate" good. This in turn will hinder your ability to connect with audiences. They may not be able to explain why you seem unrelatable, but they will *feel* it.

In its extreme form, this is upper-case "N" Narcissism (officially called "narcissism personality disorder"), which is a serious psychological disorder. Narcissists create a false reality where they are perfect, and everyone else is at fault for everything. If they have enough money or power, they accumulate a lot of yes-men and -women to protect themselves from the truth. But deep down, they know it isn't true and are fighting off the shame they feel over their imperfections. Genuine narcissists are pitiful creatures with fragile egos that require constant praise. Accordingly, the strategies that I offer in Chapter 5 for the imposter syndrome will apply to the narcissist as well.

> **Genuine narcissists are pitiful creatures with fragile egos that require constant praise.**

2. High Improvement Misalignment: Imposter Syndrome

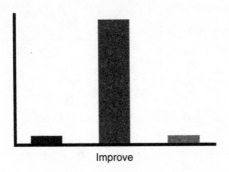

Improve

If your emphasis is entirely on improvement, you'll experience the imposter syndrome, never believing you're good enough. You'll either get discouraged and give up or else work yourself to death. Just as important, you won't be able to recognize and utilize your strengths. As I said before, StrengthsFinder is a great tool for this. (Or for a more personalized assessment tailored to you as a speaker, you can sign up for a discounted, one-time coaching session with me https://advance.as.me/assess). Again, we'll focus on specific strategies for dealing with this in Chapter 5.

3. High Acceptance Misalignment: Victim Mentality

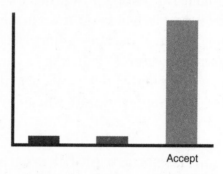

Accept

Finally, accepting everything is evidence of a victim mentality. It means you feel powerless against both your circumstances and your identity. You believe that trying to change is pointless. This belief decimates your confidence and makes you lethargic. It's a death sentence to any career and to personal growth. We'll also address specific strategies for a victim mentality in Chapter 5.

Improve or Accept?

When you have a healthy alignment, you'll see a certain progression in your life. It's like when you're younger: You enter kindergarten not knowing how to do much. You can't really read, do subtraction, and so on. As you progress through elementary, middle, and high school, you are continually improving. By the time you are college age, you should have a good sense of what you are good at, like athletics, computers, or organizing. You may appreciate these things but are trying to improve everything else. Then, as you progress through your professional life, you begin to recognize your own limits. There are certain things that you'll never be great at, so you learn how to accept them.

Another key point: Nothing should permanently remain in the improve column. Either you'll improve it and move it into Appreciate or else recognize that your energies are better spent elsewhere and move it into Accept. The only reason Improve should stay roughly equal to the others is that you need to keep putting new things into it. As you grow and mature, you'll see when it's time to improve and build on the things that you used to appreciate.

One of the most important abilities you can develop is knowing whether to assign a weakness to the accept or improve column. People often try to improve what they need to accept and accept what they need to improve.

> **People often try to improve what they need to accept and accept what they need to improve.**

Ask questions like:

- What have I tried in the past to fix this weakness? How successful was my attempt?
- Is this weakness tied to one of my strengths? My impatience, for instance, is part of being an Activator.
- Will trying to change this make me less *me*?
- Are there ways I can accommodate this weakness?
- How much work will improvement require, and will the result be worth the effort?

Your answers will help you understand if that weakness should go into Improve or Accept. As I said before, these aren't permanent assignments. You may later move them.

CONFIDENCE IN WEAKNESS

So far, the discussion has been about strengths and weaknesses in general. But this is a life-changing, confidence-creating paradigm for speakers. Here's why:

Having areas that you *appreciate* immediately boosts confidence. Going up on stage is more fun when you know that you rock the Q & A (for instance). And when someone criticizes something that you genuinely know is a strength area, you can just let it roll off your back. I worked for one place where someone in leadership constantly criticized my upfront communication style but always in vague and unhelpful terms. It could have crushed me, but I'd been doing it long enough to know it was just an issue of personal tastes. When I left there and went to another organization, they loved my style.

Then you have weaknesses you know that need to *improve*. Those don't negate your strengths nor diminish your personal value. If someone criticizes you on one of these, you can honestly say, "Yeah, I know. And here's what I'm doing to improve." As I'm writing this, one of my Improves is maintaining consistent high energy while filming my YouTube videos, and I expect to have gotten noticeably better by the time I'm done with this book. There's no ego or defensiveness involved. I need to get better, and I'm working on it.

Likewise, there are the weaknesses that you learn to *accept* and create plans to accommodate. If someone says to you, "I just watched Tony Robbins, and you are not nearly as inspiring as he was," you can say, "Yeah, I know. I'm not him. But here's my thing . . . ." For instance, I'm not any good at following all the fine details of a project. I accept that. The type of person who is into details can't do what I do. So, I accept it and find gifted administrators (and I *really* appreciate them).

So far, we've just looked at discovering who you are and how to work with it. But we are more than the sum of our innate strengths and weaknesses. We get to decide what matters to us and what we'll spend our lives on. Those decisions are what really determines our identity, and that's the subject of our next chapter.

CHAPTER 4

Your Anchors: Values and Mission

The San Juan Islands are an archipelago in northwest Washington State, considered by many to be the crown jewel of the already magnificent Evergreen State (I'm a Washingtonian by birth and a little biased). They're a very popular boating destination, and I've spent many summers boating around them with my dad. But they aren't for the novice boater. With little warning, vicious winds from the Strait of Juan de Fuca, the waterway between the Olympic Peninsula and Vancouver Island, can turn a calm day into a dangerous one (there's a reason the nearby National Park is named Hurricane Ridge).

Imagine sailing out in the San Juans and being caught in an unexpected storm. You know your boat is nearly unsinkable—as long as you don't run aground. All you can do is drop your anchor (better yet, two anchors) and ride it out. Audiences can be as fickle as the waters around the San Juans. You may give a speech and have the crowd nod along, laugh in all the right places, and applaud thunderously at the end. Then you could give the same speech to another crowd and be met with stony faces. If your identity is based on how your audience responds, you could be sailing smoothly one moment then crashing into a reef the next.

We all like to be liked, myself included. I love speaking to a group that loves me. But it's dangerous to entrust your identity to the audience because what we call "insecurity" is simply a weak identity. It is looking to others to tell us who we are.

Insecurity is simply a weak identity.

The first source of speaking with confidence is, as I've said, determining your identity. If you don't know who you are, you'll be like a boat in an unpredictable sea, riding emotional waves and blindly navigating based on the perceived reactions of your audience. (Notice I said *perceived*—that perception can sometimes be wildly inaccurate.)

If you know who you are, you'll be anchored in that truth—regardless of the audience's response or waves of doubt that splash inside you. The last chapter talked about *discovering* your strengths and weaknesses. Now we'll turn to *determining* the twin anchors of your values and mission. Regardless of what you're talking about or whom you're talking to, who you are and what matters to you will always shine through.

YOUR FIRST ANCHOR: VALUES

If I were coaching you, right about now I'd ask you to define your personal values. It's not the sort of thing that most people can do at the drop of the hat, so I have a great tool to get you started, available at content.mikeacker.com. It starts with a list of almost 700 words, such as adventure, duty, thoughtful, cheerful, honesty, maturity, and wonder. It's not an exhaustive list, and you may need to add some words, but it's enough to get you started.

The exercise begins with circling every word that describes what matters to you. Choose words that are both actual and aspirational, i.e. things that already reflect you and things you *want* to reflect you. For instance, you may be late to everything but have already added that to your "improve" column, so you decided to circle "punctuality."

That done, narrow your selection to the top twenty-four. This is crucial because you can't do or be everything. Choosing your top twenty-four helps you distinguish between the things you believe are important and the things you want to define you. For example, let's say you circled both *outlandishness* and *decorum* because you think both are important. I'd agree with you: Variety is the spice of life. But which one embodies you? People frequently struggle here because they think they *should* be one because it's more popular (outlandishness) but are more attracted to the other (decorum). If this step is a struggle, go back to the assessments I discussed in the previous chapter. They'll help you better understand and appreciate your natural tendencies.

That said, you are still choosing—determining—what matters to you. This isn't fate chiseled in stone from ages past. These twenty-four words are your way of saying, "This is who I want to be."

Great job. Now let's cut that list in half. This helps you distinguish between your high- and low-priority values. It's not that you've rejected or marginalized the bottom twelve; you've just recognized which are most important for you.

Now, cut it in half again, this time deciding which ones you want to focus your energy on. Let's say organization and risk-taking are in your high-priority values. But you know you couldn't be messy if you tried. Taking risks, on the other hand, makes you slightly nervous but calls to you at the same time. No need to put organization on your Focus 6 list, but definitely add risk-taking.

Once you know your Focus 6, then you can intentionally work on cultivating them. Ask yourself, how are your values currently being demonstrated in the following areas? How do you want them to be?

- Family
- Love Life
- Friendships

- Career

- Finances

- Recreation

- Health

- Personal/Spiritual Development

What does this have to do with confident speaking? Your true identity in everyday life must match your identity as a speaker. If your values include cheerful, down-to-earth, and acceptance, but you turn into a stiff, know-it-all college professor the moment you step on stage, it's proof that your personhood—the unique qualities that make you an individual—has been replaced by a speaking persona.

In Chapter 2, I addressed how we all have an image in our mind of how good speakers are supposed to speak and try to mimic that. But there is another factor at play, and that is learning who you are *distinct from others*. What I mean is that if you owned a hundred acres out in the middle of nowhere, you could describe your property line as "along that hill, out to the creek, and through that field." You could afford to be vague. But if neighbors start moving in and you want to build a barn in "that field," you need to know exactly where the line is or else you could end up encroaching on someone else's land. That happened to a friend of mine, and she had to pay off a very angry neighbor to keep him from ripping off the corner of her shed!

My point is that your understanding of your personhood is allowed to be vague if you're by yourself. Once you start interacting with others, you are in constant danger of encroaching on others' fields (trying to be like them) or having them encroach on yours (letting them tell you who to be). As you determine and develop your values, you are effectively bringing in a surveyor to define your boundaries.

YOUR SECOND ANCHOR: MISSION

Years ago, I was working at a large organization as they went through a massive rebranding. We hired a consulting firm to help us clarify our evolving identity. They began by digging deep into our story, values, and goals. Once they understood who we were, they were able to create a beautiful new brand and a powerful mission statement. The new mission statement didn't change us—it focused us.

I've had the honor of serving on several boards, including "GO on the Mission," a group dedicated to equipping impoverished children to conquer the cycle of poverty (visit them at www.goonthemission.com). As a board, one of our most important roles was guarding against "mission drift." There was no shortage of needs, and the caring staff wanted to help everyone. But we understood that trying to do everything would result in not doing anything very well. Every now and again, we'd have to say to the executive director, "That's a great idea, but it will pull you away from our real mission."

That's the purpose of a mission statement: focus an organization on what matters the most to them. If large organizations and successful companies know their purpose, shouldn't you? In the words of the classic Disney song "The Circle of Life," there is more to do than can ever be done. You have to determine your focus based upon your strengths and values.

A mission statement focuses you on what matters the most.

As an extension of my work as a speaking coach, I have a speakers' agency, and I've discovered that one of my most important tasks when onboarding a new speaker is helping them focus their mission and, hence, their message. So, let's say you were my client and you wanted suggestions on how to find speaking gigs.

I'd start by asking, "*Who* do you want to speak to? *What* do you want to talk about? *Why* does it matter to you?"

If you answered, "I don't care. I just want to speak," there wouldn't be much I could do to help you. Contrast that with one of my speakers. Ask him that question, and he'll say, "As a Black software designer for several international corporations, I know the feeling of being an outsider and the new kid on the block but also know what it takes to succeed. I want to speak to new hires and inspire them to take initiative and be the team members that every manager longs for."

Now, *that* sells itself! Who, What, and Why are all neatly packed in fifty-five words.

What's your mission? Even if you don't have one written out, it's probably still inside you. It's essentially the answer to these questions:

- What do you want to accomplish in life?
- What makes you feel most fulfilled over the long haul?
- What kind of legacy do you want to leave behind?
- What do you want people to say at your memorial?

Ultimately, mission is defined by action. Your mission in life is what you do, and values are why you do it. Hence, your mission must flow from your values. If your values and mission are not tightly connected, then one (or both) of them don't reflect the real you.

Mission is defined by action.

As I said earlier, my mission is "To help people realize their potential." My family also has a mission statement: "Laugh a lot. Thank God for everything. Follow Jesus." This statement flows from our family's values: enjoyment, gratitude, and faith.

LIVE BY DESIGN, NOT DEFAULT

I often talk to my executive coaching clients about leading themselves. By that, I mean living life by design, not default.

If you're like most people, you probably have a normal morning work routine that can take you from getting out of your bed to sitting at your desk without having to make any real decisions. That's not entirely bad. Routines allow us to redirect the bandwidth used on insignificant decisions (what to eat for breakfast) to more important ones (how to talk to your boss about your promotion).

The problem occurs when we use routines to make the important decisions. We'll naturally default to whatever

- . . . requires the least amount of effort.
- . . . is the most popular.
- . . . causes the least conflict.
- . . . has the loudest voice.
- . . . makes us immediately happy, regardless of long-term consequences.
- . . . other people want from us.

In *Inferno*, Dante describes the punishment of those who constantly changed their allegiances, defaulting to whatever seems most popular or beneficial at the moment:

> *I saw a banner there upon the mist.*
> *Circling and circling, it seemed to scorn*
> *all pause.*
> *So it ran on, and still behind it pressed*
> *A never-ending rout of souls in pain. . .*
> *These wretches never born and never dear*

Ran naked in a swarm of wasps and hornets
That goaded them the more the more they
fled . . .[1]

The punishments in *Inferno* always represent the true nature of the crimes: Those who live by default are doomed to run around aimlessly, always stung by the regrets of a purposeless life. Is this how you want to live, pushed around by currents of popularity and personal whims, or do you want to live by design?

Your values and mission are the anchors that keep you living by design. When you have determined who you are, you can make decisions based on what matters to you, not what is easiest in the moment or most popular.

Your values and mission are the anchors that keep you living by design.

If you don't create labels for yourself, others will label you (and you will wonder what those labels are, which leads to insecurity). If you don't determine your identity, others will try to determine it for you. If you don't know your values and mission, others will always have something for you to do. That's living by default. Living by design is saying, "I know who I am and what matters to me. I am responsible for my life." This leads to speaking with confidence because you are no longer looking for external validation.

IDENTITY SWAY

Here's the thing about anchors: They aren't meant to bind you firmly into one spot. The rope allows you to safely drift within certain limits, called your "sway." That's by design. If you were firmly anchored at low tide with absolutely no slack, the rising tide could pull your bow under.

Even as you are anchored by your personality, strengths, values, and mission, there is still room for sway in your identity. There are two aspects of these variations: the parts of yourself you choose to present in the moment and your plans for future growth.

1. Choosing the Now You

In Chapter 2, I warned against creating a speaking persona that is separate from the real you. That doesn't mean your identity and speaker-identity are the *exact* same thing. Instead, your speaker-identity should be a selective magnification of your real self.

Your speaker-identity should be a selective magnification of your real self.

Here's what I mean. Let's say that you're in the middle of an argument when the phone rings with an important call. What do you do? Take a moment to gather yourself and answer with a pleasant "Hello!"—right?

Does that mean you're being fake? Probably not. In fact, the ability to regulate your emotions as needed is an indicator of emotional intelligence. In that moment, you select *which part* of your true self to bring forward. You are normally a polite person (I hope), so answering the phone politely is really you, just not the "you" that you were feeling when the phone rang. However, if you're always yelling at home and acting nice at the office, that's what we call hypocrisy.)

This concept "which part of me" is key in speaking. Let's say you got a speeding ticket on the way to giving a speech or presentation to your team. And then, just before beginning your talk, you saw a text about a big deal collapsing. (Side note: those are good reasons to give yourself plenty of lead time and not check your phone before a presentation!) Is part of you feeling disappointed and maybe even ticked off? Probably. But another part of you is still the professional with something important to share. Which part of you should show up to the lectern? Choosing to show the angry part isn't "authenticity." It's selfishness. This is a speech, not a therapy session. Instead, you need to put on your big-person pants and give the best speech you can. As with the phone call, you aren't being fake. You're selecting which part of the real you to offer to your audience.

This is a speech, not a therapy session.

Notice that I also said, "selective *magnification* of your real self." The larger your audience, the more exaggerated your entire presentation must be. You're still you, but bigger, so that the people in back can feel you at normal size.

2. Planning the Future You

Going back a couple pages to the hypothetical where you asked me for help finding speaking opportunities and I asked you:

- *Who* do you want to speak to?
- *What* do you want to talk about?
- *Why* does it matter to you?

Let's say those questions really got you thinking, and you came back to me and said, "I'm a hospice nurse, and I want to speak to people who've just been diagnosed with a terminal illness and their families. I want to talk to them about advocating for themselves because I've seen too many patients and families feel abandoned by the healthcare industry."

Wow, I can work with that. With that end in mind, we can determine how to shape and design the future you to become that speaker while keeping it within the sway of your personality, strengths, values, and mission.

We'll look at things like how you should dress to reach that audience. You may decide to quit smoking. We'll discuss if you should highlight your professionalism or personability. We'll talk about your sense of humor and how to best use it. I'll give you skills (Section III) to focus on.

I love to quote Will Smith's character in the movie *Hitch* as he's helping a client improve his look. The client complains that a pair of shoes aren't "really me." Hitch replies, "'You' is a very fluid concept right now. You bought the shoes. You look great in the shoes. That's the 'you' I'm talking about."

Hitch wasn't trying to turn the client into something he wasn't but to improve his look and communication skills, so that the quality guy underneath could shine. So, I guess you can call me the Hitch of communication.

DEEPER THAN SHOES

I'm a coach and not a counselor, but it's interesting how occasionally I end up encouraging my clients to seek professional counseling. Maybe I shouldn't be surprised—counseling has been key in helping me reach my full potential.

In *Speak with No Fear*, my first strategy is to "uncover and clean your speaking wounds." Roughly two-thirds of my clients are hiding an emotional wound and can often point to a specific memory or event that caused it. Here's a quick test: When you think about giving a speech, do you experience a visceral fear that is disproportionate to the situation? If so, you may need to deal with that before you'll truly feel confident.

Emotional wounds do more than cause stage fright. Past traumas can prevent people from really being themselves. For example, I had an exceptionally bright client who came off to others as an airhead. Through our work and professional counseling, she discovered it was caused by the way her father always mocked her whenever *he* felt intimidated by her smarts. As those wounds healed, her real self was able to come out.

Past traumas can prevent people from really being themselves.

Again, I'm not a counselor, but if you have a deep sense that something just isn't working right inside, then counseling might be worth examining. It's absolutely nothing to be ashamed of.

———————

Living by design sounds like a great idea, but it's easier said than done, right? A host of obstacles stand in your way: imposter syndrome, fear of rejection, comparison, victim mentality. The list goes on, but we'll deal with those (and more) in the next chapter.

CHAPTER 5

Navigating the Obstacles, Part I

Standing on the beach with a surfboard in hand, I knew how to read the water. To the uninitiated, it looked like perfect waves waiting for the taking, but I knew about the hidden dangers—rip tides and currents, the raw sewage pipe, and spiny sea urchins (I'd found one the previous year the hard way—I don't *ever* want to do that again). Yes, I was able to catch a lot of great waves but only because I understood the dangers and obstacles.

I could offer you a bunch of temporary solutions, so you can *feel* more confident when you speak (e.g. "Imagine everyone is in their underwear"—one of the dumbest pieces of advice BTW), but I'm more interested in helping you *be* more confident by determining your identity. It's difficult work, and there are a lot of obstacles to navigate.

In this and the next chapter, I'm going to chart a route through the six biggest ones my clients have faced. This is going to be practical stuff, so hang on for a great ride!

1. IMPOSTER SYNDROME

You've made it "into the room" but can't shake the belief that you don't belong there and that everyone else does. You're afraid of being found out and exposed for the fraud you know you are. Never mind the fact that you have all the education, skills, and experience: You just *know* you don't belong. So, is it any surprise that your confidence evaporates when it's time to give your presentation? In Chapter 3, I connected this with a High Improvement Misalignment, so if that's a struggle for you, this section could be very helpful.

Important note for those with a High Appreciation Misalignment, that is, lower-case "n" narcissism: If you read the heading "Imposter Syndrome" and thought, *I can skip this one—that's never been an issue for me*, give me just a second here. In my experience, pretty much everyone is going to struggle with either a victim mentality or imposter syndrome. To be human is to know you need to improve in some areas and accept your shortcomings in others. For that reason, the only way to max out the Appreciation bar is to ignore your faults. Still don't believe me? Try carefully reading the "Ladder of Value" below, and if it snags something in you emotionally, then maybe the rabbit hole goes deeper than you think. Professional counseling may be helpful here. And if *that* suggestion causes an emotional reaction, consider it further confirmation.

Moving on, in my experience, the imposter syndrome can be either driven by how you feel about yourself (internally driven) or how you feel in relationship to others (externally driven). I'll deal with each separately.

Internally Driven Imposter Syndrome

It's not something I talk about a lot, but I used to be a pastor. My reluctance doesn't spring from embarrassment or losing my faith but because people tend to act a little weird around them. When I first became a pastor, I felt a lot of internal pressure to live up to everything I preached, but it's much easier to say something than do it. It was very tempting for me to start adding layers and create a pastor persona (very much like the speaker persona), that is, to become a hypocrite. I had to make a choice to strive for the standard I preached and then be honest when I failed—that last part being the hardest and most important.

Internally driven imposter syndrome is essentially feeling like a hypocrite. You've placed the layers of your speaking persona around yourself, but you know that it doesn't match who you are on the inside. The solution is so simple that you don't need me to tell you what it is: Make your inside and outside match. As I said in Chapter 2, remove the layers on the outside while building up the person on the inside. Easily said but harder to do. Use what you learned in Chapter 3 to lean into the abilities that got you the position ("Appreciate") and do whatever it takes to live up to the expectations ("Improve"). Most importantly, be honest about your shortcomings ("Accept"). Honesty annihilates hypocrisy. And if you factually know (not just feel) you lack the qualifications and have been hiding that, it's no surprise you feel like an imposter. You can either keep hiding or else come clean and fix the problem.

Honesty annihilates hypocrisy.

Externally Driven Imposter Syndrome

Externally-driven imposter syndrome comes from comparing yourself with those around you and believing you fall short. This is ultimately an issue of value. You don't feel as valuable as they are. This will make it impossible to speak with genuine confidence.

It's vital to understand that this isn't about them; your speaker identity is about you and how you perceive your own value. No one can make you feel less valuable without permission. For that reason, I want to offer you a new paradigm, a new way of understanding, that will allow you to understand your true value—independent of those around you.

No one can make you feel less valuable without permission.

Ladder of Value

I believe that there are five sources of value. These five form the rungs on the ladder of value, ascending from the least important. That is crucial to understand: You do not need the lower rungs to get to the higher. You don't even need the first one though many people gain it after reaching the others.

a. What You Own

There is some value in your money and possessions. Many people mistakenly make it to the top rung and judge everyone (themselves included) based on the car they drive, the house they own, and the money in their accounts. In reaction to that shallowness, we're inclined to say that what you own doesn't have any value. But it does. Having a house allows you to host people and create connections. I have a friend whose boat has opened all sorts of opportunities. A large bank account can be used to contribute to many valuable causes.

Furthermore, people will make assumptions about you based on what you own. If I drive up to be the keynote speaker at a conference in a Lamborghini, people will believe that I'm really successful (even though I could have just rented it for show). But that's also part of why I always wear a nice suit to professional events. It helps communicate my success as an author, speaker, and coach.

So, yes, what you own is a source of value, but it's the bottom rung and the most fragile. Someone else will always have more than you, and your possessions can disappear overnight—as we are reminded with every recession and bubble burst. Money is ultimately just a tool for accessing things of greater value.

Money is ultimately just a tool for accessing things of greater value.

b. Where You Come From

Your familial, ethnic, cultural, and national identity are part of who you are and give you value. In America, where we prize individualism over the community, we tend to undervalue this rung. But in other cultures, your community is central to your value, so much so that Socrates chose death over exile.

A word of clarification: Where you come from *is* part of your value, but it adds no more or less value than coming from a different place. Being an American gives me a certain value but no more than being Indian, British, or Mexican.

Your education is part of this value. If you graduated from an Ivy League school, that adds value. Coming from a long line of Ivy league graduates adds value and gives you opportunities that others don't have.

If the other people on your team attended a prestigious college and come from an established pedigree, but you are the first person in your family to attend college, let's be honest: That gives them a value you don't have, *but* it's only a second rung value and not much sturdier than "what you own." Having to struggle against your background just to make it into the room gives you a more important, third rung value. And remember you don't need the first and second rung to reach the third.

c. What You Have Accomplished

Everyone can reach this rung. It's the first one that reflects who you really are and what actually matters. In all likelihood, this is how you got into the room and in front of your audience. Even if everyone else has more money in the bank and more letters behind their name, something on your résumé demonstrates that you belonged there. When people ask why they should work with me, I point back to what I've done. Spoken to X-sized crowds, written all those books, coached these high-level leaders, blah, blah, blah.

What you've done adds value to you. Maybe you graduated earlier than your coworkers or were promoted to an executive role at a young age. Or maybe you overcame great adversities, and tenacity is part of what makes you, *you*. My story of overcoming a speech impediment, growing up in another culture, and struggling with my own emotional wounds is key to the work I'm doing now.

I always thought that this was higher up on the ladder, but what you've done just isn't as important as the next rung. Honestly, I don't like that—sometimes I wish I could just coast on my experience!

d. What You Are Doing Now

Your second-greatest value comes from the work you are doing now and the unique contribution you are currently making. This rung is exponentially more important than the ones before. People may hire me because of my past experience, but all they really care about is what I do for *them* in the present. What you've accomplished may have gotten you into the room, but it won't keep you there. Even if your past successes got you the job, your present performance allows you to keep it.

Understanding your identity, particularly your strengths, is crucial here because we have a tendency to compare ourselves at our weakest point to someone at their strongest (we'll talk more about comparisons shortly). For example, maybe you feel less valuable than a coworker who is far more energetic than you and is always chosen to speak for motivational events. But maybe you were hired for your insightful analysis, which is why *you* are always brought in for brainstorming meetings.

**Don't compare yourself at your weakest point
to someone else at their strongest.**

One of my clients noticed he didn't have an issue with the
imposter syndrome when working with his team but really struggled when presenting his team's research to the executive leadership. As we worked together, he realized that he was hired to do
exactly what he was doing and belonged in the boardroom meetings for that purpose. I worked with him to develop grounded-
affirmations to counteract his fears (we'll talk more about
that shortly).

The important thing about this rung is that it's the only one
you can do anything about at this moment. By reading this book,
you're already working on it. Rather than allowing the imposter
syndrome to *paralyze* you, use it to *motivate* you to push further
and harder. Just make sure it pushes you in alignment with your
genuine identity (which is why this chapter had to come at the
end of the Identity section).

If you feel like you don't belong in the room, this is your
first actionable item. Ask yourself:

- What am I doing right now?
- How am I improving myself?
- What am I learning?
- How am I adding to the value of the team?

Maybe you don't own much because of bankruptcy. Maybe
you don't have any pedigree or your past business attempts failed.
Now, you have to walk into a room with all these entrepreneurs
who are very successful and you're asking, "Do I belong?" The
answer doesn't lie in your past but in your present. You can
belong in that room on the basis of what you are doing now.

e. Whom You Belong To

Even if you *don't* belong in the room, even if somehow you got a job that is beyond your abilities, even if you were fired tomorrow, you'd still have a higher value. Your ultimate value doesn't come from what you have or have done but whom you belong to. As I indicated above, I come from a faith tradition—Christianity. I believe that my highest value comes from being a child of God and belonging to him. That's a value we all share. I believe I've been adopted into his family and am part of a church community that grounds me.

Even if you and I don't share this perspective, you are still part of a network of people that give you value. In my office bookshelf are copies of best-selling books I've written and books written by my clients. None of them matter nearly as much to me—nor communicate as much about my personal value—as a little frame, hand-painted with splotched and clashing colors, that says, "Dad." *That* is first-rung value!

If you have all the possessions and pedigree, if you've had great success and continue knocking it out of the park but don't have any real connections and feel as if you don't belong, you'll only be as valuable as your current performance or past successes. Friends, family, and faith are the three components of this rung, and they sustain you even when the four others fail you. When I've had people try to tear me down and devalue me, I turn back to my network of friends to build me up. When I start doubting myself and feel like a failure, my wife reminds me that I am hers and she loves me regardless of how many books I sell or how many times I feel that I've failed. Then my son jumps up in my lap and snuggles with me. And when I feel as if I don't measure up as a friend, husband, father, or person, God reminds me that I'm his, and that is enough.

These are the things that provide me with my greatest source of confidence. Even if everyone else in the room seems better than me, it doesn't matter because of whom I belong to. Because I know my value outside the room, I am secure in my identity inside the room.

Knowing your value outside the room causes you to be secure in your identity inside the room.

Your greatest value in life is not what you have or what you've done, so don't give up top-rung value to gain the lower ones. That's way too common and (I admit) a constant temptation to me. Making good friends, spending less time at the office to connect with family, and unplugging for extended periods to connect with something bigger than yourself can be some of the best antidotes to the imposter syndrome.

2. VICTIM MENTALITY

I just associated the High Improvement and High Appreciation Misalignments with the imposter syndrome. High Acceptance Misalignment is then associated with a victim mentality.

(Note: I want to acknowledge that many of my readers have suffered some truly horrible things, and I'm not in any position to offer any sort of mental health advice. I'm an executive and communication coach, and my advice is based on what I have lived, studied, and seen work for my clients. My goal is to help you deal with the obstacles that prevent you from speaking with confidence, but that may require digging deeper than this book can take you.)

In Chapter 3, I defined a victim mentality as feeling powerless against your circumstances and believing you can't change. *Scientific American* says, "Those who have a perpetual victimhood mindset tend to have an 'external locus of control'; they believe that one's life is entirely under the control of forces outside one's self, such as fate, luck or the mercy of other people."[1]

Accordingly, victim mentality is associated with blaming all your shortcomings on everything and everyone but not yourself. Not sure if that shoe fits? Here are some other questions:

- Do you believe that the deck is always stacked against you? That most people have things easier?

- Do you have trouble dealing with changes or setbacks?

- Are you a perpetual pessimist? Quicker to see the negative than positive?

- Do you believe that no one understands you?

- Are you hyper-vigilant for the next bad event, and do you tend to jump to the "worst-case scenario"?

- Do you hang out with people who also like to blame and complain?

If you answered "yes" to many of these questions, the first thing I want to say is this:

I'm sorry. Really, I am. A victim mentality frequently develops as a coping mechanism against trauma or extreme hardships, particularly in childhood (when you truly were a victim). If you grew up in an unhealthy situation, blaming others may have helped you survive. But what may have helped you then is holding you back now.

There's an old saying, "The same sun that melts the wax hardens the clay." The same hardship may cause one person to crumple and the other to thrive. The key difference is resiliency—the ability to recover from difficult circumstances. In her book, *The Gifts of Imperfection*, Brené Brown talks about the importance of resiliency and says the first step for building it is developing hope.

Hope is not an emotion but a mindset. It says, "I have the ability to improve my situation." Going back to what *Scientific American* said, you have to change from an external locus of control to an internal one. That means you have to see yourself as having control over your own life and to understand that, even if you can't always control your circumstances, you can always control your response to them.

Hope is not an emotion but a mindset.

This is easier said than done. From a very young age, our brain creates channels in our gray matter that allow us to perform certain functions without conscious thought. We use the term "muscle memory" to describe how continual practice allows us to type, eat, or dance without giving the individual commands to our hands and feet, but that's a misnomer. It isn't our muscles but deep pathways that we have developed in our mind.

This same dynamic happens with our thoughts; we create *mental ruts* that we run through without thinking about it. It's like the Oregon Trail, where tens of thousands of covered wagons traveled a well-worn path across the United States. Ruts developed in the road that were so deep that escaping them was nearly impossible. In that same way, we can be trapped in mental ruts of our own making. For instance, if you had some kind of traumatic speaking event at a young age (what I call speaking wounds), the resulting rejection or fear caused a deep mark in your impressionable young brain and created the belief that you are bad at speaking. You carry this belief into your future speaking events, which then steals your confidence and hijacks your presentation. This in turn reinforces the "I am bad at speaking" narrative. Each new negative event makes the rut deeper, and you'll probably start adding new narratives like "people don't like me" or "I'm bad at communication."

You can't meander your way out of these mental ruts. It requires intentional effort. The following are four vital steps to take.

a. Want It

There's a story about Jesus meeting a man who couldn't walk and asking him a strange question, "Do you want to be well?"[2] Obvious answer, right? Yet the man responded with excuses. In the story, Jesus heals him anyway, but the man continues to demonstrate a victim mentality. Jesus's question was profound because it demonstrated that fixing the external problems is pointless if we don't want to change the internal ones.

> **Fixing the external problems is pointless if we don't want to change the internal ones.**

A victim mentality is a very safe and comfortable rut to stay in. You don't have to take responsibility for your life. Others (aka "enablers") will try to help you and solve all your problems. You'll face less criticism and lower expectations if people think you're struggling. Most importantly, this mindset protects you from confronting your underlying issues, which is really scary.

Getting out of the rut is hard and painful, but I have a lot of hope that you can do it. Why? Because you wouldn't have picked up this book otherwise. So, here is what I want you to do:

- Make a list of all the reasons you *want* to stay in your victim mentality. Be honest. This is only for you.

- Read that list as if you were that "tough love" friend. What is your counterpoint to each reason?

- Now, make a list of all the reasons you want to shed it. Don't neglect how it will feel emotionally (e.g. "I won't feel shame when . . . .").

- List all the potential benefits, such as new leadership opportunities springing from your increased confidence.

- Finally, imagine yourself post-victim mentality and write out a description of how you will feel.

Do you see what you're doing? You're creating hope. You're creating a clear vision of a better future. The road ahead of you may be painful, but reviewing that vision will give you the motivation to persevere.

b. Address the Root

If your speaking wound is relatively isolated, that is, not intertwined with other trauma, you may be able to handle it on your own. I spend a chapter on this in *Speak with No Fear*, but the short version is to journal about your wounds. If that goes well, give a speech about them, maybe as a vlog or to a speaking club like Toastmasters. Sometimes just exposing the wound is sufficient.

If your victim mentality goes deeper, I really encourage you to work with a therapist or counselor. Chances are, it has held you back in many areas, so dealing with your pain could turn your life around in many areas.

c. Seek Out Positive Influences

People with a victim mentality tend to surround themselves with other victims who won't call them out. They are likely to read posts, watch shows, and listen to music that soothes them rather than motivating them to move forward. I'm not judging. In high school, I used to listen to Pearl Jam and think about how much my life sucked. Sounds a little melodramatic now, but life often *was* hard for me back then, being the only white kid in a Mazatlán school and a frequent target of an older and larger bully. But my "solution" created an ever-deepening mental rut. Thankfully, a mentor challenged me to get out of that rut by filling myself with messages that encouraged me.

Surrounding yourself with better influences may mean spending less time with negative friends and more with positive ones. Carefully evaluate your social media engagement. I have a childhood friend whose wife joined a Facebook support group for ADHD spouses after he received his diagnosis. She quickly discovered that it was more of a *complaining group* than a support group and realized it only made her resent her husband more, so she quit the group and blocked the more toxic participants from her account.

Don't just remove negative people. Evaluate everything you watch, listen to, and read. Does it fill you with hope and empower you? If not, replace it with encouraging messages. Read memoirs of overcomers, like Maya Angelou's *I Know Why the Caged Bird Sings*. Listen to podcasts that help you see what is right in our country. Maybe even watch movies like *Braveheart* that motivate you to take on the world—FREEDOM!

d. Use Personal Affirmations

You might be rolling your eyes right now, and if you're old enough, you might be thinking of Stuart Smalley in the *Saturday Night Live* sketches saying, "I'm good enough, I'm smart enough, and, doggone it, people like me!" That used to be me (the one rolling his eyes, not Stuart Smalley) until I remembered that one of the tools a former counselor gave me while I was a teenager was to look in a mirror and say "Mike, I like who you are." And it worked!

I talk a lot more about affirmations in my book *Prepare to Speak* and don't want to repeat that content. Instead, I'll set them in the context of speaking with confidence. If being a victim has become part of your identity, then you've created that deep mental rut that says things like, "I'm a bad speaker. It's the hand I was dealt, and I can't change it. People don't want to hear me talk.

They like so-and-so better." It's a loop that plays over and over in your head.

As I said before, you can't ease out of that rut. You need to take decisive action to pull yourself out. That requires replacing an unhealthy mental rut with a healthy mindset. An affirmation is nothing more than 1) determining what you want to be true of you—based on your values and mission—and then 2) affirming (defined as "expressing agreement with or commitment to") it on a regular basis until it displaces your old rut.

Psychology Today offers four helpful guidelines for creating your own affirmations:[3]

1. Take ownership by beginning them with "I . . ." or "I am . . . ."

2. We are more motivated by positive statements than negative, so don't use "no" or "not."

3. Don't neglect the heart—use emotive words. For instance, "I feel proud of every presentation I give."

4. Write them in the present tense, as if they are already happening. We believe what we say and say what we believe.

We believe what we say and say what we believe.

Want it, address the root, seek better influences, and use personal affirmations. These aren't magic solutions but a straightforward path to taking responsibility for yourself and growing as a speaker and as a person.

3. LIMITING BELIEFS

Just like your values, your beliefs drive what you do and what you think you're capable of. You've collected them, usually subconsciously, from your family, culture, and personal experiences. Sometimes, they empower you and push you forward. Sometimes, they limit you and hold you back. Becoming a confident and powerful speaker requires that you examine all the beliefs that have been limiting you.

Becoming a confident and powerful speaker requires that you examine all the beliefs that have been limiting you.

There are two types of limiting beliefs. The first type includes broad beliefs about life in general. Consider your gut-level answer to these questions:

- Is being rich usually the result of hard, honest work or using people?

- Is it acceptable to be outspoken among your peers? Your superiors? What if you're a woman?

- Is it better to fit in with everyone or stand out?

- Is being well-spoken and more intelligent than other people something to hide?

- Does being popular and well-liked mean you are shallow?

- Is it okay to be proud of your success?

- Is making a mistake and apologizing for it shameful, or is it refreshing?

This list could go on much longer, but you get the point. You have deep-seated beliefs about what sort of things are acceptable and praiseworthy. Those beliefs may provide you with a moral compass, or they may limit your ability to succeed.

The second type of limiting beliefs are the ones that you have about yourself and what you can and cannot do. These have a profound impact on you. If one of your beliefs is "I can't ever become a great communicator—mediocre maybe, or even tolerable, but never great," then you won't be! Think about other personal limiting beliefs. When was the last time you said one of the following:

- I'm not good with names.
- I'm too busy.
- I can't afford that.
- I'm not good in front of people.
- I'm always late.

A limiting belief is basically giving yourself a pass on something. They're like a milder form of victim mentality, but instead of affecting your entire outlook on life, they are confined to specific areas. They occur when you prematurely assign an "improve" weakness to the "accept" column. They can all be summed up by saying, "I'm just not good at _____."

Maybe it's true. Maybe you aren't good at that thing. There are lots of things I'm not good at. What makes one of those things a limiting belief? When they limit your ability to live out your values and accomplish your mission.

Here's what I mean. Because my mission is "to help people realize their potential," I have no problem leaving my receding hairline and tone-deaf singing in the accept column. But "I'm not good at names" or "I'm too busy to talk" limits my ability to accomplish my mission. Remembering names and finding time for people are difficult for me, but I can't give myself a pass on them, so I've developed strategies to overcome those challenges.

What are beliefs that are limiting your ability to be a confident speaker? Take some time to list them out. In my experience, these are the most common ones:

- I'm not good at humor.

- I get lost in my thoughts and lose my audience.

- I don't have a good voice for speaking.

- I can't get rid of using fillers (umm, extra words, etc.).

- Others are just better than me.

- I've always been bad at speaking.

- I tried in the past, and I didn't improve.

- Introverts can't be good speakers.

Some of these simply are not true (e.g. many of the best speakers I know are introverts). Others are just a matter of learning better techniques. Yet others require creating workarounds. For instance, my editor is also an experienced speaker, but he's dyslexic. He avoided reading in public for the first half of his life, but that limited his ability to speak, so he taught himself to semi-memorize anything he'd need to read in a speech.

Over the next week, try to record your limiting beliefs. Watch for all the times you think or say, "I'm not good at _____." Notice all the little ways you give yourself a pass on something. As you read through your list, you'll notice that some are just weak excuses. "I'm too busy," for instance, is a weak way of saying, "Everything else I'm doing is more important to me." Highlight these ones, and then try this tactic: Create a modified version of a swear jar. Every time you use a weak excuse, drop in a dollar.

Take the remaining limiting beliefs and evaluate each one. Which ones are false and simply need to be corrected? Which ones do you want to move to your "improve" column? Which ones require new skills or strategies? Which ones are deep-seated cultural beliefs that you no longer want to hold? Those can be the hardest to change and require intentional and consistent effort. For instance, if you grew up hearing intelligence belittled, you'll need to intentionally contradict that belief. Whenever you notice that you're hiding your abilities, silently remind yourself, "Being smart is good."

It all comes down to this truth that Henry Ford taught us, "Whether you think you can or whether you think you can't, you're right." You can be a *great* communicator. You can make it part of your identity.

"Whether you think you can or whether you think you can't, you're right."

CHAPTER 6

Navigating the Obstacles, Part II

T he previous chapter covered three obstacles that are largely driven by what you think about yourself. These next three are more about what and how you think of others.

1. YOUR VERBAL AND MENTAL TRACKS

I've been told that the average person talks at between 100 and 150 words per minute (good or bad, I'm on the high end of that) and think about 500–600 WPM. With that kind of difference, it's not surprising that there are always two tracks running in our heads, even when we're in the middle of a speech or presentation. The verbal track is what we are saying at 150-ish WPM. Then there is all the stuff going on in our head, the mental track.

This is unavoidable, but our brains are able to multitask to some degree (technically, we never multitask, just switch tracks rapidly). Incidentally, the better you have prepared for your presentation, the easier it is for the mental track to separate from the verbal one. If you think of it like train tracks, there's no problem with having two tracks—as long as they're both headed in the same direction. It's when one goes left and the other right that we have a problem.

Now, as an experienced speaker, I know how to occasionally let the mental track run ahead separately, using it to better communicate and connect with my audience. I'm able to pay attention to dozens of little clues and make micro adjustments, all without my speech ever being derailed. Even then, both my tracks are continually pointed toward the audience. But that comes from years of experience. For now, I want you to focus on keeping your mental and verbal track as close together as possible, and here's why: Your mental track will naturally stray to thinking about yourself instead of the audience.

Picture this. You're giving a presentation that you've rehearsed several times, so your verbal track runs along at a full 125-ish WPM. No longer fully occupied with your next sentence, your mental track starts noticing everything else. You hear the little mistake you just made and wonder who else heard it. Someone yawns, and you nervously speed up to 160 WPM. Someone else's eyes drift down from your face, and then they grin suddenly. You wonder if your fly is down and can't stop thinking about it. Your mental and verbal tracks have parted ways, and whenever that happens, the verbal track will always lose.

Whenever your mental and verbal tracks part ways, the verbal track always loses.

Notice what the mental track was focusing on: *you* and not the audience. Everything you thought led back to "What do they think of me?" instead of "Am I communicating effectively?"

As I said, it is possible to read the audience and make adjustments to increase their understanding, but this isn't nearly as straightforward as noticing a single yawn (maybe he stayed up all night taking care of a new puppy at home) or a grin (maybe she randomly remembered a meme she'd seen that morning).

I learned a lot about what you can and cannot learn by reading an audience when I was still a pastor. There was one guy, someone I really respected, who always slipped out the back door whenever I got up to preach. It really rattled me. I wondered why he didn't like me, and it started to make me doubt my identity as a speaker. Finally, I worked up the nerve to talk to him.

"Hey Fred," I said. "I don't want to make a big deal out of it, but I noticed you always leave just as I'm getting up to preach. Have I done something to offend you?'

Fred's eyes widened. "Oh my gosh! I didn't even think about that . . . . No, I leave early because I work on Sundays and didn't want to interrupt you in the middle of the sermon."

I also learned how easy it is to misread nonverbal clues. I've had people who seem completely checked out but can later repeat what I said verbatim. And you shouldn't read too much into what people say either. I learned that when a new person said, "That was the best sermon ever! I love this church!" it usually meant I'd never see them again. Can't tell you why; that's just the way it was. That's why I say reading an audience is not a reliable science, so I don't recommend it for beginning speakers.

Even if you're reading the clues correctly, that doesn't always mean you should change course. I once attended what I thought was a networking meeting, but it turned out to be a sales presentation. That's enough to put anyone in a bad mood. I tried half-heartedly to be polite as he pitched his product, but all my nonverbals were saying, "I don't want to be here and am not remotely interested." The salesman expertly ignored all that and persevered (to be clear, he hadn't been sneaky—there was a communication breakdown on someone else's part). Slowly, his consistent excellence and content won me over. It was a really good opportunity that he was selling. Long story short, the one guy who was giving off the worst nonverbals (me) ended up being the only one to sign up. I can't know for sure, but I'm guessing that salesman's mental track had been screaming, "Abort! Abort!" the whole time, but he stuck to his plan, and it paid off.

I know it's hard to ignore the verbal and nonverbal clues that your audience seems to be giving. One of the biggest causes of insecurity in communication comes from the uncertainty of communication. You don't know how your message is being received, and that steals your confidence.

The insecurity of communication comes from the uncertainty of communication.

While I could give you some tricks to reading a crowd, it's more important to stop looking at the audience to give you confidence. The crowd can be a very fickle thing. Don't focus on their reaction but on your identity as a speaker and your prepared message (more on that very soon). As I said in Chapter 3, there have been some people who don't like my communication style. If I focused on making them happy, I'd cease doing what I do well *and* do a lousy job of what they want. But because I know who I am, I focus on being the best speaker I can be.

In good time, you'll learn how to use your mental track to improve your verbal one, but for now, focus on keeping them as close together as possible. To do that, try using "nudges" to push the tracks back together. A nudge is a little like an affirmation but only two or three words long, short enough to say to your mental track without messing up your verbal one.

The most basic nudge is "Back on track." You can practice it in everyday conversation. When you notice your verbal and mental tracks separating, don't get down on yourself; just say "Back on track." If you practice in everyday life, it will become natural to use in the middle of your presentation.

Next, pay attention to the places where your mental track tends to stray when you speak. For instance, I teach my clients how to be confident in their message (we'll get to that in the next section) and not doubt themselves during the presentation. Calling an audible mid-talk is almost never a good idea. So, if your mental track tempts you to adjust your material based on a random yawn, use the nudge "Don't doubt." Your mental track won't need any more than that. It will know what you mean. Or let's say your inner critic loves to hijack your mental track. "Shut up" is a very appropriate nudge to use on *that* jerk.

As another example, I believe that a speaker should always be focused on serving their audience (we'll talk about this in Chapter 9). I may choose my speaking engagements based on *my* mission and values, but once I arrive at the venue, it's completely about *them*. Because of this, I hardly ever think about myself or what the crowd thinks of me. I focus on helping them, which in turn eliminates self-consciousness. Sometimes, however, my mental track tries to put the focus back on me. At that point, a nudge like "Serve them" is a great way to refocus.

The trick to keeping your mental and verbal tracks close together is never focusing on distractions or beating yourself up for slips but using little nudges to move on without dwelling on them.

2. Comparison and Competition

Two big obstacles to confident speaking are competition and comparison. Comparison is like competition, but *in absentia*— you can't literally compete but do so figuratively from a distance. They are both naturally destructive to confidence but can be used to build it up when used properly. Starting with comparison, there are three different kinds, but only one is helpful:

a. Losing Comparisons

This is when you compare yourself to some other speakers, like a famous TED speaker, and say, "I'm not as good as them. I could never stack up against that." Then what happens? You're flooded with self-pity. Victim mentality kicks in and kicks out your confidence. You simply stop trying. As I said earlier, we tend to compare ourselves at our weakest points to someone else in their strongest.

Social media is notorious for this. You see your coworker's vacation picture, and it's a perfect Instagram moment. She looks perfect, her husband gazes at her admiringly, and her kids are angelically grateful to be on a Mexican beach at sunset. #nofilter? Yeah, right. That picture gives such a narrow slice of a bigger story that it's essentially fake. As I write this, Facebook is in a lot of hot water for the way it uses losing comparisons to drive discontent and increase advertising dollars. Who wins when we compare ourselves like this? No one—except the advertisers.

Even if that photo is an accurate depiction of her life, that doesn't factor in all the areas where you are stronger than she is. This goes back to Chapter 3 and learning to value your unique skills and abilities.

b. Winning Comparisons

If you're feeling down (maybe because of too many losing comparisons), there's nothing like Googling "people of Walmart" to make you feel superior. Or try reading about some celebrity's relational train wreck. There will always be someone you can look down on to puff yourself up. But can you see what's happening here? You're comparing yourself at your strongest to them at their weakest.

Even without social media, we do this all the time—use winning comparisons to build our confidence. But they don't build confidence; they *inflate* it. And anything easily inflated will deflate just as easily. Furthermore, winning comparisons lead to hubris, and audiences hate hubris. Instead of connecting with your audience, you'll be separated from them by all the false air that hangs about you. No matter how humble you act, people will see right through you.

c. Learning Comparisons

I once went to an event with a friend where the speaker was impressively awful. I was knee-deep in winning comparisons and leaned over to make a sarcastic comment to my buddy, but he was taking notes! I whispered, "Man, you could *give* this speech way better than him, without even trying."

His response? "I can always learn what not to do." He didn't say it with a trace of arrogance. He was humbly learning from his comparison.

Likewise, there's a saying, "You don't know what you don't know." My team regularly compares my website to better ones to gain new ideas. I'll listen to world-class speakers and read great books to help me speak and write better. I don't change my identity to fit theirs but look to learn new perspectives and ideas. This type of comparison builds confidence because I'm improving my toolbox and getting better at being my ideal me.

Turning now to competition, it can also build confidence or destroy it. Last year, my son started playing T-ball, and his team was the second-best team in their league. I couldn't be happier about that placement. Having a team that was better than them energized them. It pushed them to work and try harder. They played at their very best against the number one team, and thanks to that, my son was one of the best players on his next team.

Competition serves a vital role in pushing us further than we'd go on our own. In my book *Connect Through Emotional Intelligence*, I say we need to have some level of competitive relationships in our life to motivate us. Healthy competition is going toe to toe with someone who is as good as (maybe even a little better than) you, pushing both of you to do even better. I've been at places where I'm the best speaker on the program and at others where I'm in the middle of the pack. One is good for my ego; the other is good for my performance. Those two are mutually exclusive by the way.

Good for your ego and good for your performance are mutually exclusive.

Unhealthy competition isn't about being better but being better than someone else. Even if you do improve, the focus is still on you, not communicating and connecting better. Your skills may go up, but your relatability will go down.

The real difference, however, between healthy and unhealthy competition comes down to *identity*. Unhealthy competition is the result of having your value and self-worth attached to your performance. It's like Jaime Tartt in the first season of the show *Ted Lasso*—he doesn't know who he is if he isn't the best player on the team. If your identity is secure, it won't matter if someone is better than you because "you" isn't determined by them.

Here are some questions to help determine if your competition is healthy or unhealthy:

- Would you rather be the best player on a mediocre team or a mid-list player on a great team?

- Are you still you if you don't win?

- Can you learn from those you compete with?

- Can you celebrate their wins?

If you don't like your answers, go back and study the "Ladder of Value" at the beginning of this chapter. Here's what you need to remember: There will always be someone who is a better speaker than you, whether it's someone in your office (competition) or you see on the internet (comparison). This truth can either drive you to improve or be an obstacle that shipwrecks your identity.

3. REJECTION

I was twenty-six when I was selected to pastor my first church. Looking back, that feels way too young, but I'd already been their associate/youth pastor for four years, was well-liked, and had been endorsed by the outgoing pastor. The final phase of the selection process involved me giving a sermon followed by a congregation-wide vote. As I sat in the front row waiting for the board to count the votes, I was mentally confident of the outcome but was emotionally nervous.

The chairman of the board finally entered the room and approached the podium. "By near-unanimous vote, Michael Acker has been selected as our new pastor." I didn't have any time to wonder what "near-unanimous" meant because four people promptly stood up and walked out. This was a small church, the kind of place where everyone knows everyone, so their conspicuous departure sucked all the excitement out of the room. Those four people knew that I was sure to be approved. Why had they even come that Sunday? For the sole purpose of publicly rejecting me.

Every one of us has faced rejection and will face it again. The reason most people fear public speaking is that they fear rejection. While that fear is almost always exaggerated greatly, any kind of public speaking—from giving a speech, to making a sales presentation, to leading a meeting, to toasting your best friend at his or her wedding—risks disapproval. I don't have any tricks or techniques for preventing rejection, and even if I did, I wouldn't give them to you because I believe that there are incredible benefits to being rejected.

That sounds weird, doesn't it? I'm not saying I *hope* you'll be rejected. I don't enjoy rejection any more than you do. But it's a vital part of developing confidence because untested confidence isn't bravery: It's bravado.

Untested confidence isn't bravery: It's bravado.

My son recently came back from the neighbor's house visibly upset, just minutes after he'd left. The neighbor boy was playing with another kid and didn't want to play with my son. Part of me wanted to storm over there—anyone who rejects my son will feel the full wrath of his father! But on a deeper level, I knew that my responsibility wasn't protecting Paxton from ever being rejected but teaching him how to be resilient and learn from it. In fact, this is the best possible time for him to face rejection. He lives in a stable home environment where he is well-loved and accepted. He has parents who can help him process his feelings and grow.

I'm going to give you four ways rejection can make you a more confident speaker, followed by six things to do when rejected.

a. Rejection Pushes You to Work Harder

I'm a big Seattle Seahawks fan, so here's to all the 12s out there! The Seahawks "Legion of Boom" was one of the most powerful defenses in the NFL, as seen in their 43-8 victory over the favored Denver Broncos in Super Bowl 48 (but don't talk to me about Super Bowl 49). What a lot of people don't know is that none of the Legion were first-round draft picks. Russell Wilson, our star QB, was a 75th pick overall, and the Seahawks were widely condemned for wasting their third round on him. If it ever seemed like the Hawks played with a chip on their shoulder, it's because they did. All of them felt like they'd been underrated and undervalued, so they pushed themselves insanely hard to prove their critics wrong. Rejection will either make you give up or try harder: Practice more, read more books, invest more in your success, seek more opportunities, and risk more.

b. Rejection Makes You Go Deeper

What I'm talking about here is character and what you're made of. This is the "when the going gets tough, the tough get going" type of stuff. Rejection will force you to reach deep down inside and say, "This is who I am, and I'm not giving up!" It's where everything I said about values and mission in Chapter 4 is proven. It's easy to say that you value honesty until you face rejection for telling the truth.

c. Rejection Forces You to Try Smarter

When you are rejected, it means something didn't work the way you wanted it to. That's an invitation to try again, smarter. Entrepreneurs rarely succeed on their first attempt—in fact, none that I can think of. Like many of you, my world was thrown out of balance during the COVID pandemic, but I used that as an opportunity to try something new. My first idea didn't work. My second didn't either. The third sort of worked. I just kept on trying and getting more creative.

As you grow and stretch yourself as a speaker, you're going to try new ideas, new skills, new tools. Some of them may work the first time, but some won't. When something fails, your temptation may be to say, "I'm never going to do *that* again," but it's better to say, "Okay, that part of it worked, but the rest was a mess. How can I fix that? What can I do smarter?"

d. Rejection Makes You Grow Tougher

Confidence in speaking, leadership, and life requires a thick skin. Did I want the vote to accept me as pastor to be unanimous, instead of nearly unanimous? Of course, but that's unrealistic. You will always face rejection and criticism. Some of it will be justified and constructive; some of it will be unjustified and destructive. Either way, you must have the ability to face it without crumpling. This is part of what is meant when I talked about resiliency. One of the tricks of any profession that cares for people, from first responders to pastors and counselors, is learning to have thick skin but a soft heart. The same is true of speakers. If you absolutely cannot handle rejection, then you'll never be a confident speaker. Calluses are crucial for confidence.

Calluses are crucial for confidence.

The best salespeople aren't the ones who experience the least amount of rejection. They frequently experience the most but have calluses that allow them to focus on the goal. Great salespeople know that every "no" gets them that much closer to the next "yes," and I want all of us to develop that skill because speakers are basically in sales. We have a message that we want others to buy into. Whether you are a CEO, politician, pastor, or presenter, or are interviewing for a job, you're in sales and you need to develop a salesperson's calluses.

So, the four ways that rejection can make you more confident are pushing you to work harder, go deeper, try smarter, and grow tougher. Easy, right? Of course not, but here are six things that can help you get there.

a. Establish a Personal Refuge

As I said earlier, now is the best time for my son to experience rejection because he's in a really safe environment—a refuge—where he's unconditionally loved and can process his feelings. In the same way, I can handle a lot of rejection out in the marketplace because I'm accepted at home. We need a healthy place where we are loved, so that we can respond to rejection in a healthy way.

I really hope you already have that. If so, lean into it. This means being emotionally vulnerable and letting others know when you need encouragement. My wife, Taylor, is both my most trusted advisor and greatest comforter, but sometimes I need to clarify which role I need. When I share my frustration over a presentation that didn't go well, she may start offering some really helpful suggestions. Sometimes, that's great. Other times, I'll say, "I just need encouragement."

If you don't have a place like that, create one. It can make the difference between building you up or tearing you down. Look at your current networks and relationships to see if any of them are ready to go deeper and become a supportive place. Find a good counselor, coach, or mentor that can provide you with a better perspective. I was recently reading through some new reviews on one of my books. The vast majority were positive, but then I read, "It's obviously something that the publishing company just paid someone to crap out on the page." What!? I felt like an innocent pedestrian being hit by a garbage truck. I have over 500 five-star reviews, but that one was all I could think about. Then I brought it to a network of professionals that I'm a part of, and they were able to give the perspective I needed to both take it in stride and learn what I could from it (we'll get to that).

b. Grasp Your Real Worth

Why did that negative review hit me so hard? Because I took "your book is worthless" to mean "*you* are worthless." We are all incredibly prone to confusing who we are with what we do. You are not what you do—you have great worth and value separate from that. Resiliency in the face of rejection requires a firm foundation of your real worth. Go back to the "Ladder of Value" in Chapter 5 and write out all the reasons you are valuable. Keep that in front of you to remind yourself that your life is so much bigger and richer than any presentation or speech you give.

You are not what you do.

One of the most important things I do as a communication and executive coach is help my clients battle insecurity by finding their real worth. Yes, rejection feels personal, and the bigger it is, the more personal it feels. But if you're secure in who you are, you'll know that you aren't the rejection.

c. Hold to Your Mission and Values

Similarly, knowing your mission and values is crucial for taking rejection in stride. As I said in Chapter 4, they are the twin anchors that hold you firm in the midst of the storm. There will always be plenty of people making all kinds of demands on you, and you need to have a clear understanding of what is important to you. For example, if your values include being easy to understand and relatable, then you can safely ignore someone who complains that you don't sound scholarly enough. More than ignore them, you can take it as praise. I like the question my editor asks before working through my book, "Whose rejection would be a compliment?" A question like that leads to fearless writing and speaking!

Too many people lose sight of where they're going when they experience rejection. It makes them focus on the moment. It makes them doubt their goals and question their progress. It tempts them to give up. Never abandon an established mission because of a passing criticism. This is another great reason to have a written mission and value statement. If you know where you're going and refuse to be sidetracked, no amount of rejection can stop you.

> **Never abandon an established mission because of a passing criticism.**

d. Foster a Positive Mental Attitude

We are not machines, and even if you follow all the above advice, rejection can still wear on you. But at the end of the day, the only person responsible for your attitude is you. You have to be your own greatest supporter. You have to be the person encouraging yourself when it feels no one else is. How? By being intentional about the influences you allow into your life. Read encouraging books. Listen to motivational podcasts; for instance, check out mine at podcast.stepstoadvance.com. Find music that gets you charged up. This is not the place to be passive. You have to fight for a positive mental attitude.

e. Imagine the Worst

This is my second strategy in *Speak with No Fear*. Surprised? It's like FDR said, "We have nothing to fear but fear itself." It's a bit of a hyperbole, but it reminds us that our fear of a thing is usually worse than the thing itself. If you clearly and carefully think through the potential rejection you might face, you'll frequently find that the worst-case scenario isn't that bad. Just as important, you'll be able to prepare yourself to handle those possibilities. A lot of the fear of rejection is driven by "what ifs." What if they laugh at me? What if there's a heckler in the audience? What if my fly is down? Think through as many of those as you can and create backup plans.

f. Learn a Lesson

I love what John Maxwell says, "It doesn't matter if you fall down, as long as you pick up something from the floor when you get up." I've learned as much from the mistakes I've made and the rejections I've faced as all the things I've done right.

> **"It doesn't matter if you fall down, as long as you pick up something from the floor when you get up."**

I intentionally placed this last because you won't be ready to learn from rejection if you don't have the other pieces in place:

- If you don't have a refuge and aren't fostering a positive attitude, rejection will overwhelm and paralyze you.

- If your worth is in what you do, any rejection will be far too personal for you to evaluate objectively.

- If you aren't holding on to your mission and values, rejection can throw you off course.

After those four people walked out, I made a point of connecting with them. I knew each of them personally and had thought of them as friends up until then. The meeting did not go great. It mostly involved their spokesperson criticizing me. As much as I wanted to defend myself, I saw an opportunity to learn. I knew my value didn't come from their approval, so I could just listen and gain valuable lessons, and some that are still a part of me today. But when the spokesperson started to repeat herself and I knew the meeting wasn't going anywhere, I ended it. I still knew who I was, and their rejection hadn't turned me into something else.

Rejection is not fun, and I don't look forward to whatever forms it will take next, but I am grateful for what it can do in me. I hope that you can see rejection as an opportunity instead of an obstacle. Here's a little bit of homework for you: Put yourself out there and take a risk. Do something that's not a sure thing. Talk to your boss about the responsibility of being a presenter at the next event. Ask that person on a date. Try to hire away that star player. Ask for a promotion. Reach out to your favorite author. If they say yes, awesome! If they say no, then lean into what you've learned here.

———————

You are the message. Everything you say is filtered through your personhood, so gaining confidence in who you are will revolutionize what you say. But you still have to say *something* up at the lectern. In the next section, I'll build on the foundation of identity and teach you how to convey your message in the best way possible even when speaking off the cuff.

PART II

DEFINE
THE MESSAGE

CHAPTER 7

The Elements of a Confident Message

O ver the years, I've given upward of 3,000 talks, sermons, presentations, and speeches. My audiences have been as many as 10,000 over a weekend and as small as one person. Some of the ones that stand out the most are my mom's memorial service, a prayer vigil after a mass shooting in my small community, my first workshop for a group of executives, and certain sermons that changed people's lives. What do these have in common? I had something important to say to people who really wanted to hear it.

In the first chapter, I compared your identity to a boat and your message to the cargo that in it. These, along with the skills it takes to handle the boat, are the three sources of confidence. In this section, we'll focus on creating messages that allow you to speak with confidence.

Imagine that you're seconds away from giving a speech and can truthfully make all these statements:

- I'm passionate about my topic on a very deep level.
- I've researched my topic thoroughly and am an authority on it.
- I've studied my audience and its needs, and I've planned specific ways to connect with all of them.

- My audience is interested in my topic and is eager to hear my presentation.

- My speech is well-written and structured effectively.

- I finished writing it ahead of time and have been practicing it.

How do you think you'd feel? More confident, that's for sure. Maybe even a little eager and excited. Speeches like this can be fun to give.

Now, imagine that this is your reality instead:

- I couldn't care less about my topic.

- I'm not confident in my topic and hope I gathered enough info to hide my ignorance.

- I don't know anything about my audience and their needs.

- My audience ranges from uninterested to hostile.

- My speech makes a drunken rant look organized.

- I'm still writing my speech as I'm being introduced and haven't practiced at all.

Just *writing* that makes me feel anxious (and it brings back memories of some of my train wreck–level speeches). A hostile audience can drain the confidence of all but the most experienced speakers. A lack of preparation is the reason we have dreams about showing up at school in our underwear. Notice these elements of a confidence-building message:

1. A personal investment in, and thorough knowledge of, the topic.

2. A connection to, and understanding of, the audience, including their interest and needs.

3. A speech that is organized, well-written, and well-practiced.

A speech that checks all these boxes comes with built-in confidence. It won't be enough to remove all doubts (you still need identity and skills), but it will make a massive difference. Here is a crucial point to understand: This is not an all-or-nothing scenario. You do not have to check off every box in order to speak with confidence. Many of them may be out of your control:

- Your boss may "ask" you to give a presentation on a subject that is less interesting to you than dirt or a topic you actively dislike.

- Maybe you talked your way into a position that you aren't quite ready for (we've all done it) and are still learning about your topic.

- You may have to give a presentation "blind," that is, without any information about your audience.

- You may have to speak to a group that wants you to fail.

- You may be thrown into a Q&A session without warning.

None of them are deal breakers because every box that you can check off will increase your confidence. Control what you can control, and don't worry about what you can't. So, if you're a politician getting ready to talk to the opposing side, but you understand them, know your topic like nobody's business and are passionate about it, and are well-prepared, you can still enter that town hall with confidence—especially if your identity is already well-grounded.

Control what you can control, and don't worry about what you can't.

The rest of this section will equip you with the tools you need to build a message that inspires confidence (in you and your audience). I'll start by talking about some of the fundamentals of building a good speech and then move on to systems that will help you work as efficiently and effectively as possible for any type of speaking occasion.

CHAPTER 8

The What: Your Content

One of the most frightening moments in the life of any teacher or speaker—or parent—is when they realize the audience believes what they're saying. With that influence comes a lot of responsibility. At the same time, one of the most exciting moments is when they see a life changed by their words.

A past client of mine, Glenn, was a middle manager at a tech company. He was an incredibly capable guy when it came to spreadsheets and logistics. His ability to think through problems had gotten him a promotion, and he loved the new responsibilities (and bigger paycheck), but he was terrified by the management meetings. Just the threat of being called upon to speak sent him running for Tums. Giving a presentation felt like an insurmountable mountain. On the nervousness scale, he was easily up there at a nine or ten. Maybe you can relate.

Glenn did everything he could to avoid the weekly Zoom meetings, including feigning sickness and tripping the breaker on his Wi-Fi router. But he knew that his lack of confidence would rob him of all chances of further promotion and maybe even cost him his current position. Glenn showed more courage than most by facing his fears and reaching out to me. The first time we met, he could barely look at the camera, and I had to keep asking him to speak up.

Over the course of our sessions together, I talked to him about things like his identity and knowing who he was. We focused on his message and the reality that he had far more to offer than he gave himself credit for. We worked on specific skills that increased his confidence. If I could show you our first and last coaching sessions, you'd have a hard time believing it was the same person. The same guy who faked sickness to avoid being called upon was now volunteering for every speaking opportunity and asking his boss for more. That is my favorite part of my work. I love seeing my hard-won message change the lives of my clients.

Your belief in, and connection to, your content increases confidence. A lot. It also brings excitement and creates the pathos I talked about earlier. The rest of the chapter will cover key components to building that connection to your message.

SOMETHING TO SAY

At the center of every speech, presentation, or meeting is the content of your message. You have something to say, and it is the reason you're so eager to speak with confidence. The name of my speakers' agency is Audacity Speakers, followed by this explanation:

> Why Audacity Speakers? Because powerful speakers have one thing in common. It's not a particular style, but firm confidence that they have a message to share and value to provide. We call that audacity.

Catch that: not a style. All my speakers have very different styles—from bubbly and infectious to slow and thoughtful—but they all have the confidence that springs from the message that they are passionate about.

Perhaps, at this point, you're thinking, *That's great, but I just give sales presentations, not a TEDx speech. Maybe I should skip ahead a bit*. You could do that, but you'll miss out on one of the most important sources of confidence: caring about your message.

Caring about your message is one of your greatest sources of confidence.

Obviously, this is easier for some topics than others. I care way more about helping people with their identity, message, and skills than walking them through the mechanics of my program—how to log in, Zoom links, and making sure they're comfortable with the entire process, and so on. For that reason, I'm always tempted to "phone in" the orientation but remind myself that a better understanding of the mechanics results in higher participation, resulting in more growth for my clients. The key is to connect the orientation with its purpose.

Here's another example of connecting seemingly insignificant content with purpose. When I was the chairman of the board for GO on the Mission, I cared a million times more about lifting kids out of poverty than understanding *Robert's Rules of Order*, but I quickly discovered that they were essential for running the organization in an orderly and legal manner. Connecting *Robert's Rules of Order* with taking care of the kids made me care about motions, seconds, and tabling discussions. Connecting content with its purpose increases passion.

Connecting content with its purpose increases passion.

If you struggle to care about your topic, connect it back to its purpose. Maybe the sales figures can help your team sell more of a product you believe in. Maybe the new IT protocol will prevent a ransomware attack. Maybe killing it with those ROI presentations will ensure that you survive the next round of layoffs. That's a cause you can get excited about, right?

Or maybe your newly acquired passion for the "Workplace Safety Orientation" will help that new kid take it seriously and save him from a life-altering (and lawsuit-inducing) injury. That really is a purpose worth caring about.

FIND THE PURPOSE

Purpose. That's the starting point of every great speech. We talked about purpose on a macro level in Chapter 4. Your mission and values represent your personal purpose, the *why* that drives the *what* you do. In the same way, every talk needs to have a purpose. You cannot give a presentation until you know why you are doing it.

You cannot give a presentation until you know why you are doing it.

This may seem obvious, but you'd be surprised at how often people are in so big of a hurry to work on the *what* that they skip the *why*. And by people, I mean me. As an activator, I'm eager to get Project A done, so that I can start on Project B. My editor, Josh, is annoyingly relentless about purpose. I'll routinely send him some of the best content in the world or a document full of material for a website, but he won't work on a single sentence until he knows my goals. Annoying, but important. He knows (and I concede) that the best written words are useless if they don't achieve the desired results.

Knowing the purpose is vital for distinguishing between the means and the ends. Have you ever seen a commercial so hilarious that you posted it on your feed but couldn't really remember what it was advertising? The producers confused the means (entertainment) with the end (selling a product). Your message has to be built around a purpose, which creates a very straightforward metric: Did it accomplish the stated purpose?

In Chapter 6, I said that one of the biggest causes of insecurity in communication comes from its uncertainty. At that point, I was talking about the uncertainty of how the audience was receiving your message. This statement is even more true of the message itself. Being uncertain of what you're trying to say, and why it matters, breeds insecurity. Confidence in the purpose of your message creates confidence in the message itself.

Confidence in the purpose of your message creates confidence in the message itself.

CLARIFY YOUR POINT

What is the main idea? Every talk, speech, or presentation needs to begin with its point. Notice that I said "point," singular. One speech, one point. It's that clear. And if it's that clear to you, it will be clear to your audience.

Said another way, if a person who skipped out on your presentation texts their more responsible colleague, "Wht mtg abt?," what answer would you want them to give? That is your point. Think very carefully about that and keep it in front of you as you write your message (we'll talk more about this when I show you my systems for writing).

A lot of my past clients have struggled accepting this. They don't think there is any way they can "confine" their subject to one idea. They're sure that they can be the exception. Years of communication have taught me this truth: Most people will only take one main point away from your speech. They may be able to remember a sub-point or two, quote a statistic, but in their mind the speech or presentation was about one thing. It's like when you ask a friend about a movie or TV show. They'll either summarize it down to one main thing or say, "You have to watch it for yourself." You have no power over the human propensity to simplify and summarize. The only thing you have power over is the likelihood that *their* "one thing" will match *your* "one thing."

Most people will only take one main point away from your speech.

Again, we're going to talk more about constructing a speech that clarifies the point, but for now, I want to make *this* point very clear: Confidence is directly proportional to clarity. A laser-focus on the one thing you want your audience to gain will cut through all the confusion in your head. It also marshals your passion into a focused purpose.

Confidence is directly proportional to clarity.

So, how do you find your one point? Easy. By going back to the purpose. It is not the same thing as the purpose but rather a point crafted to accomplish it. For instance, let's say that your purpose is getting your department to adopt email practices that protect your company from ransomware. That's a great purpose, but it isn't actionable. So, this might be your point: In order to shield yourself from personal liability that could run into six figures, never, ever open any attachment without first doing XYZ.

The point is the actionable item that accomplishes the purpose, that is, "Never, ever open any attachment without first doing XYZ." Notice also that it appeals to the listener's personal interests: "Shield yourself from personal liability." We'll cover that in the next chapter, but specific, personal interests are more persuasive than general, impersonal ones.

So, you know the purpose and point of your message. It's something you care about. But do you know enough to talk about it? Uncertainty about your topic is another major cause of insecurity.

BE THE AUTHORITY

It's called the "Dunning–Kruger Effect." People with low ability or expertise in an area tend to overestimate their ability, and people with high ability or expertise tend to underestimate it. You've probably seen this in action: The people who know the least are frequently more confident than those who know the most. Why is that? Because those who *do* know have a keener sense of how much *more* there is to know.

Your lack of confidence in your message may be evidence that you are the best person to deliver it. The fact that you have been asked to give the presentation is *prima facie* evidence that you know your topic and suggests that your fears are unfounded. I see it happen all the time—people who feel unprepared to talk about something, even though they literally are experts. Sometimes I have to say, "Stop researching! You already know more than your audience could possibly take in."

Whenever you're preparing for a presentation, carefully assess the audience's knowledge of the topic vs. yours. Not yours vs. other experts in the field. Not yours vs. your professors. Only look at yours vs. your audience's. Again, you probably know more than you need.

Another confidence buster I've seen in my clients is being fixated on the audience's knowledge of *other* topics. The only question is what they know about *your* topic. If your area of expertise is wastewater treatment, you can confidently give a presentation to Bill Gates about that. Just don't try bluffing your way through. Highly competent people can see through BS even if they don't know the topic. And avoid straying into computers or business management because Bill will take you to school there.

However, if your assessment reveals that you don't know as much as you need, it's time to do some research and remedy that problem. Feeling unprepared is one of the most anxiety-inducing things I can think of. Think of it like this. I recently did some landscaping and needed beauty bark. The nursery said it should be 3/4″ thick, but that gets expensive, so it's tempting to go for the bare minimum needed to cover the ground. You could get away with half that—for a little while. As soon as there's some wind or rain, the shallowness will show through. Same thing goes for research. Only being an inch deep does not breed confidence. Knowing significantly more than you plan on saying, however, keeps you covered and confident.

My rule of thumb is that I want to know three to four things for every one thing I say. So, if I'm giving a 30-minute speech, I want to know enough to talk about the subject for 90 to 120 minutes. That way, if I rush through faster than antici-pated or get a lot of questions, I'll still have plenty of "fill-in" material and the audience won't be able to blow through my layers of knowledge. I don't want to be like the contestants on *Shark Tank* who are left staring dumbly at the investors after just a couple rounds of questions.

My most non-intuitive principle for confident speaking is that you should always feel at least a little fear (I talked about this at the end of Chapter 1). Second might be, "The audience doesn't care about you as much as you think they do." In the next chap-ter, we'll look at how that truth reduces insecurity.

CHAPTER 9

The Who: Your Audience

I said in the previous chapter that the center of any message is its content. No content, no message to speak. But the reason for every presentation is the audience. To play off of a classic philosophical question, "If a speaker gives a speech and no one is around to hear it, does he or she make a sound?"

The reason for the presentation is the people, but they're also the reason for most of the fear. Think about it. Fear of public speaking is driven by (1) the challenge of gathering and organizing the content and (2) the prospect of having to present this content to real people. Some people fear creating the message more, but most are more afraid of the audience. The percentage of each person's fear driven by the audience varies, but I have a very scientific method to determine your percentage. Just answer this question:

How much would you prefer to deliver the content via an email over a live presentation? Mark your answer below.

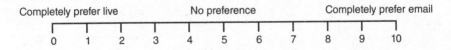

Completely prefer live   No preference   Completely prefer email

0   1   2   3   4   5   6   7   8   9   10

Got it? Now, find the number below your answer and multiply it times 10. That's the percentage of your fear that is driven by the audience instead of the content. So, if you marked a 7, then your fear is 70% audience. Maybe this isn't quite *that* scientific.

Knowing your percentage will help you focus your efforts on what is the greatest threat to your confidence. Based on my experience, chances are good that your percentage is somewhere north of 75%. This is why I spent so much time on "Identity." The more secure you become in who you are and what matters to you, the less the audience will matter . . . . Wait, I said that wrong. The more secure you are in your identity, the more the audience will matter to you, but in the right way. Let me explain that next.

The more secure you are in your identity, the more the audience will matter to you.

THE AUDIENCE ISN'T THERE FOR YOU

Unless we're talking about family or friends who have come for emotional support, the people in an audience never show up for the sake of the speaker. They are always there because they want something. They aren't there for you; you are there for them—quite literally. For several reasons, understanding this is crucial for speaking with confidence.

1. They Aren't Thinking about You as Much as You Think

It's easy to imagine that they're noticing every single mistake and waiting to pounce on every misstep. Sure, there are a few jerks out there, but most people are too busy thinking about themselves to focus that much on you.

2. They Want You to Succeed

Have you ever paid good money for a concert hoping that the artist would fail? Do you go to a speech hoping it will be boring and hard to follow? Not unless you already have some sort of grudge against the speaker. Your audience wants you to do well, not only because of empathy (which is also a huge factor) but also because they want to gain something from you. It's your job to give it to them, but they really hope you succeed.

3. It Changes Your Focus

In Chapter 8, I talked about Glenn and his journey to increasing his confidence. He developed his own set of affirmations and nudges (Chapter 5). This is the one he used whenever he felt his anxiety rising: "Focus on them and not you." He discovered that by focusing on the audience, he thought less about his fear. Why is that? Because insecurity is self-focused. Its only concern is "What are they thinking about *me*?" Focusing on yourself increases fear; focusing on serving others decreases it. Glenn discovered that when his focus was on serving the audience, there was less left for insecurity.

> **Focusing on yourself increases fear; focusing on others decreases it.**

4. It's More Fun

You're heard the saying, "It is better to give than to receive." Studies have backed this up: We experience joy when we give. When your presentation is all about *you* receiving positive feedback from the audience, you'll not only miss out on the joy of giving to them, but you'll also discover that they can never give you enough to make you feel secure. I'm going to repeat that: An audience can never give you enough affirmations to make you feel secure.

When my identity is well-anchored and I know that my message could literally change someone's life, I can't wait to give it like a gift. Even if the message isn't life-changing but simply helps them do their job a tiny bit better, the joy that comes from focusing on the audience is still far greater (and more substantive) than the pleasure of hearing, "Good job!" This is a soapbox of mine: The goal of the speaker is always to serve the audience. It is not their job to serve me.

The goal of the speaker is always to serve the audience.

RUNNING RECON

I think this is obvious enough: If you're going to serve them, you need to know who they are. Most of my clients do almost all their speaking to people they already know. If that describes you, this and the following two sections ("Points of Connection" and "Talking to Individuals, Not a Crowd") may not be as relevant, but you'll still find a lot of useful ideas. And who knows when you'll be called on to represent your company at a civic event?

It's hard enough speaking to people you know but even harder to strangers. Simply by doing your homework and studying your audience, you can greatly increase your confidence. Find out everything you can. Study their website; learn about the organization. Interview the facilitator. Here are some of the questions I try to get answered before writing my speech:

- How many people will be in the audience?
- Are they accustomed to interaction and participation?
- What is their temperament as a group?
- What are their expectations for the event?
- Is the audience excited about the topic?
- Why are they going to be there? Is it required or voluntary?

- What do they know about me and my presentation?
- What motivates them and affects them?
- What are their demographics—average age, education, socio-economic status, ethnic background, religious and political affiliation?
- What are their fears, hopes, and aspirations?

Also try to learn more about the history of the organization. How were they founded? What are their values? What are the stories that they tell newcomers? You may not be able to get every question answered, but each answer will allow you to better prepare and set your mind more at ease.

POINTS OF CONNECTION

The ancient Greek word for hospitality is *philoxenia*, from the word for friendship-love (*philos*) and the word for stranger (*xenos*, as in xenophobia). Hospitality turns the stranger into a friend. A good speech is an act of hospitality—inviting a crowd of strangers to become a group of friends. By using the information you learned above, you create points of connection with all in your audience and turn them into friends. This is a huge confidence booster.

Points of connection are simply anything that you hold in common. It doesn't need to be a huge commonality. For instance, if you're speaking to a company that prides itself on hiring vets and you're a vet, that's a no-brainer. But if you're not, you might briefly mention that your favorite grandfather always taught you to honor those who served. Of course, if you come from a long line of pacifists, this may not be the time to mention it. Instead, look for a different point of connection.

A word of caution: Be very careful about being overly familiar. People love finding points of connection but hate outsiders inviting themselves in without permission. A lot of Michael Scott's social blunders in *The Office* are based on this. The more hard-won their membership, the truer this is. So, if you're talking to a group of Army combat vets, don't say anything like, "My dad was in the National Guard for six years, so I know exactly what you've been through. I mean, he was never deployed, but still . . . . Oorah!" Seriously, don't do that (especially since "oorah" is a Marine thing, not Army). Always undersell your connection and allow them to invite you in. So, you could say, "My dad was in the National Guard, and he never went through what you did, but his respect for combat vets definitely wore off on me."

Nothing connects better than something that honors your audience while poking fun at yourself. A great example comes from *Walk the Line*. Joaquin Phoenix, playing Johnny Cash, is doing a concert at Folsom Prison. Speaking to the crowd of cheering inmates, he says,

> You know, standing back there in your shop, catching my breath, I come to admire you even more. You see, I never had to do hard time like you although I have on occasion gotten myself busted. Once in El Paso, I had this bag of—[loud cheering]—oh, you heard about that?
>
> Well, anyways . . . . I felt tough, you know? Like I'd seen a thing or two. Well, that was till a moment ago because I got to tell you—my hat's off to you now because I ain't never had to drink this yellow water you got here at Folsom.

Notice that he finds a point of connection and demonstrates his acceptance (especially important to inmates who were used to being judged) but is careful not to claim his own place among them. And the entire time, he honors them and shows respect.

Nothing connects better than something that honors your audience while poking fun at yourself.

Another way to create points of connection is to find examples and analogies that are relevant to their industry or office culture. So, if you discover that your audience has a huge March Madness office pool, then maybe use an NCAA underdog story as an illustration. But I'd encourage you to run your ideas past your contact person in advance.

Connecting through your research of all the audience also creates instant credibility because it says you've done your homework and are interested in them. You don't have to become an expert in their field (and don't try to pretend that you are), but if you can demonstrate that you understand their unique setting and challenges, they'll take your message more seriously.

In addition to finding points of connection, researching your audience allows you to tailor your speech to the specific needs of a new audience, which is key because your goal is to serve these people, right? We'll talk more about meeting needs shortly.

TALKING TO INDIVIDUALS, NOT A CROWD

Which is easier to speak to, an individual or a large crowd? An individual, of course, but a crowd is nothing more than a large group of individuals. It's only when you get enough of them together that they become a faceless crowd. Finding points of connection will help you relate to them and understand them better, but they are still a crowd.

Learning to see them as individuals is one of the greatest confidence boosters that I know. Whenever I speak at a live event, I always arrive with plenty of extra time to complete my preparation and then hang out with the audience. My goal is to create a personal connection with three to five individuals. When everyone starts taking their seats, I pay close attention to where my new friends are sitting. As I mentally prepare to go on stage, I remind myself that I'm not talking to a room of strangers but to a few friends. And if I ever feel myself floundering, I look to them. Speaking to a crowd is scary, but speaking to friends is fun.

Speaking to a crowd is scary, but speaking to friends is fun.

Here are some of my tricks for making that connection. First, remember that being the speaker or presenter automatically gives you permission to talk to anyone. It's kind of like being a professor or the CEO—no one thinks it's weird for them to strike up a conversation. There is a certain confidence that can and should go with the position.

Second, have some icebreaker questions in your "back pocket."

- What's your role in this organization?
- What's your favorite part about working here?
- What are some of the challenges you face?
- What are you hoping to gain from this?
- Where are you from?
- What about you is most surprising to others? (This is a great one for bringing out some fascinating stories.)

Third, if you've done your research, you can also prepare some audience-specific questions, like "If I understand correctly, this company_____. Did I get that right?" It's also a good way to test out some of your connection points from the last section and gauge how effective they are.

Here's a pro tip for you: Never pass up an opportunity to eat with an audience. There's something about eating that brings out a sense of hospitality (turning strangers into friends) in people.

What if your presentation is virtual? That makes it harder but not impossible. Again, doing your research in advance helps. Having a couple Zoom meetings with your contact person is also a good idea. Then see if you can get the guest list and use LinkedIn, Twitter, and Facebook to learn more about a few people. I also like to log on early and chat with some folks prior to starting. Again, you don't have to get to know everyone. Just enough to make it feel personal.

Maybe, at this point, you're thinking, *I'm an introvert, so this doesn't apply to me at all.* I disagree. Where you are on the introvert/extrovert scale will affect *how* you connect with people, but making a few friends will still help you speak with greater confidence. In fact, you may need it even more than the extroverts. You just need to adjust your technique. In my experience, introverts will do better connecting with fewer people at a greater depth. Also, consider stocking up on "social bandwidth" by not doing anything too social in the days prior to your speech.

WHAT DO THEY REALLY, REALLY WANT?

I've checked into enough hotels that my mind often wanders when they start going through their whole thing—damage deposit, no smoking, and on it goes. But when they tell me where my room is, what time breakfast is served, and how to log onto the Wi-Fi, they have my full attention. We are interested in the things that benefit us. That's human nature, and you can make it work for you because few things build confidence like having an audience that hangs on your every word. All you have to do is give them information that they really, really want.

We are interested in the things that benefit us.

You start with a purpose, like we talked about in the previous chapter. You may be able to craft the purpose, or it may have been given to you by a supervisor or the event facilitator. Then you have all the audience, and they have their own purpose for being there. As you study them, keep these questions in front of you: What is their purpose? What do they want? Not what their boss thinks they should want, but what they actually want.

Dale Carnegie famously said, "Arouse in the other person an eager want. He who can do this has the whole world with him." While this can be done manipulatively, Carnegie didn't mean it that way. Instead, he was encouraging us to pay attention to what others want and appeal to that. If your sales presentations or safety talks can consistently make life better for your audience, you will quickly find yourself becoming the most popular speaker even over those who are more "entertaining."

Think about your purpose and look for the place where it intersects with your audience's needs. In other words, how can your stated purpose

- . . . improve your audience's lives?
- . . . help them become healthier, emotionally, relationally, and physically?
- . . . make them feel better about themselves?
- . . . help them make more money?
- . . . increase their sense of security?
- . . . protect them from the uncertainties of the marketplace?
- . . . help them enjoy their work more?

Said another way, you must tie the purpose back to why the audience should care even if that reason is "so you don't lose your job." When you can answer those questions, you'll be able to create a message that your audience is eager to hear. Then, as I discussed in Chapter 8, use this information to craft a point that will resonate with your listeners and create a receptive audience.

Understanding all in your audience, serving, and connecting with them, giving them something that they really want. These are all ways you can use to improve your message and increase confidence. This chapter and the previous have focused on the fundamental questions of *what* you are saying (the content) and whom you are saying it to (the audience). With that foundation in place, I will turn to some of my most practical material, beginning with systems that will allow you to craft your content into more powerful communication in less time—or even in no time at all (i.e. my "Off the Cuff" system).

CHAPTER 10

The Power of Systems

Some of the best "Eureka!" moments occur at the collision of two seemingly unrelated concepts. That's exactly how the original eureka story took place. Ancient math–whiz Archimedes was contemplating a hard-to-prove theft while taking a bath when he came up with the idea of measuring volume via displacement.

My eureka moment about systems wasn't as historic as Archimedes', but it can significantly improve your ability to construct better speeches faster. Instead of his collision of a crime investigation and personal hygiene, mine brought together the concepts of speech writing and franchises.

When I first started as a public speaker, it took me up to twenty hours to write a speech. With each new speech, I essentially had to start from scratch, and it ate up huge chunks of my week. I was highly motivated to find a better way. Through trial and error (and practice), I was able to develop a personal method that cut that time down to four to six hours for a thirty-minute speech—while increasing quality. Sound farfetched? Keep reading.

As my workload increased, I hired Jimmy to oversee one of the departments, and this responsibility included his having to give regular presentations. He was a hard worker and eager to learn, but I noticed that he frequently wasn't completing all of his week's duties or was staying at the office far too late. When

I asked him about it, he said that he ran out of time because he was preparing for his presentations.

"How long does it usually take?" I asked.

"I don't know, twenty hours?" Jimmy said.

I was sympathetic, but we couldn't afford him spending that much time on speech writing, so Jimmy became one of my first "clients," and he quickly learned how to cut it down to four to six hours.

As I've pivoted into professional coaching, I always ask my clients how many hours they spend preparing. Some of them are like Jimmy and spend far too much time. Others of them answer, "Zero. I just wing it." Then I think of their rambling, pointless, please-shoot-me-now talk, and I think, *Yeah, I can tell*. It's like when someone asked Woodrow Wilson (the U.S. president during World War I) how long it took for him to prepare a speech. He responded:

> It depends. If I am to speak ten minutes, I need a week for preparation; if fifteen minutes, three days; if half an hour, two days; if an hour, I am ready now.

A good speech, like the kinds I've been talking about, takes time to craft. But it doesn't have to take as long as most people think. I've had great success teaching my clients proven methods to consistently develop powerful presentations in a quarter of their previous time. That's the first concept behind my eureka moment.

Apart from my passion for communication, I love starting things. It's the Activator in me. I especially love franchising things—taking successful endeavors and replicating them elsewhere. Inspired by the book *The E-Myth Revisited* (by Michael Gerber), I've "franchised" churches, feeding centers, and businesses.

At the heart of effective franchises are systems. Systems are what happen when effective policies meet a flow chart of the "If A happens, do X, but if B happens, then do Y" variety. They basically give the new franchisees all the tools they need to replicate your success. I once consulted for a company in southern California where we systematized every single thing it did, from the way it contacted clients to how it dealt with complaints. No matter the situation, we had a playbook for it, and if we didn't, we'd make one. That's not exactly accurate—if something just happened once or twice, it could be an anomaly and not worth the effort. I like what Chandler Bolt, founder of the highly systemized Self-Publishing School, said. You should create a system for anything that you (1) have to do more than three times or (2) want to hand off to someone else.

Systemizations are key to franchises for three reasons. First, they create consistency. Starbucks may not be the best-tasting coffee in the world, but that's where I go when I'm in a new town because I know what to expect.

Secondly, they make it easy to hand something off to someone else with a minimum of management (making systems unpopular with micromanagers and control freaks).

Finally, systems prevent you from having to reinvent the wheel every time you perform any given task. By investing extra effort the first or second time to understand the problem, developing a long-term solution, and documenting it in an accessible manner, you will save everyone a considerable amount of time in the long run. With proper training and empowerment, others will be able to customize the system for new (but similar) situations.

That is to say, I love systems. They've allowed me to accomplish more at a higher level with less effort, giving me time to start more new things! So, the second concept behind my eureka moment was systems.

Here is how the concepts of systems and speech writing collided. While I was still consulting for that Californian company, I decided to write a book. As I said, I'm always starting something new. The book was basically about how to write great speeches in less time. I started writing out all the things I'd learned and the methods I taught to my team members and clients.

Eureka!

My messaging methods were simply new systems—I just hadn't been calling them that. I had effectively franchised myself by giving my clients playbooks on how to give presentations, write speeches, lead meetings, speak off the cuff, conduct Q & As, and more. By using my speaking systems, they eliminated redundancies and cut their preparation time down to a fraction of what it had been.

Systems eliminate redundancies.

Building on this understanding of systems, the rest of this section will be dedicated to giving you some of my best speaking systems. This in turn will dramatically increase your confidence. How? I get to repurpose a quote of mine a third time here:

The insecurity of communication comes from the uncertainty of communication.

Earlier, I applied this to uncertainty about how the audience is responding to your presentation (Chapter 6). Then, in Chapter 7, I applied it to the uncertainties around the meaning and purpose of your message. Now, I'm applying it to the uncertainty of crafting your speech. There's no need for me to prove this point. We've all experienced that soul-crushing, stomach-churning, despair-breeding experience of staring at a screen or notebook filled with worthless half-sentences and aborted openings as the clock ticks ever closer to the deadline.

Ugh. If I never have to go through that speechwriter's block again, it will be too soon. I don't want to go all infomercial on you here—"...and if you use my handy, dandy system, you won't ever have to again!"—but it's kind of true. Not that you'll never face writer's block, but you can learn to consistently craft great presentations, speak off the cuff effectively, and stop rambling. With each new win, you'll gain more confidence in the ability that I believe is already inside you.

By learning these straightforward systems, you'll be able to bypass the uncertainty of the blank page and dive write in. I mean dive *right* in. You'll become comfortable with the process: Start with "A," add "B," brainstorm "C," and onward.

Before we get started, here are some important notes:

First, like any new habit, these systems may not feel natural at first. They take practice. Just believe that they've helped many others before you and trust the process.

Second, after you master each system, you can tweak it and make it your own. Use what you know about your strengths and weaknesses to customize them for yourself. For instance, if you naturally excel at extemporaneous speaking, you might be able to reduce your notes to singular words. If, on the other hand, you do your best thinking when the pressure is off, you may want to create more detailed notes.

Third, these systems are not comprehensive. It's beyond the scope of this book to give a playbook for every kind of speaking opportunity. There are simply too many, and in some cases, I already have a book that covers that system in depth. Pay attention to the process, and create your own system for any type of presentation you expect to give more than a couple of times. Better yet, talk to someone who has done similar presentations, and see if they already have a system of their own (even if they don't call it that).

Fourth, a system is not a boilerplate where you fill in the blanks with updated names and figures. It is a format for writing new content in an efficient way. Think of two weddings you've attended, one where it's obvious the couple found i officiant via a Google search and the other where it's equally clear that the officiant has known the bride and groom since childhood. The Google officiant will use a boilerplate service, but the long-time pastor will be able to write a service that draws off years of past weddings while still being very personal. That's a "wedding service system" (and, yes, I have one of those).

Finally, franchises and systems are more focused on consistency and greatest return of quality on the lowest investment of time. As I said before, Starbucks may not be the best coffee you'll find and not even their marketing team pretends otherwise. However, I believe that people don't need the perfect answer; they want a good, solid, and helpful answer. I'd prefer to give ten great speeches than one perfect one. I say that to preemptively address common criticisms of system-based writing, such as calling it formulaic (yes, it is formulaic . . . that's the point). Just as there are formulas for great screenplays that make a lot of money (even if they don't win an Oscar), there are formulas for very effective speeches and presentations. Plenty of directors are happier with the title "box-office leader" than "award-winning," and if I was a director, I'd be one of them. The goal isn't an award-winning speech but great presentations that you can give with confidence.

However, I believe that people don't need the perfect answer; they want a good, solid, and helpful answer.

As you could probably guess, I have systems for almost everything (and I'm always developing new ones). All of my books are essentially codifications of some of my systems, including:

- *Speak with No Fear*: Systems for alleviating paralyzing fear.

- *Lead with No Fear* (written with Steve Gutzler): Systems for courageous leadership.

- *Grow Your Soul*: Systems for restoring your spiritual life.

- *Write to Speak*: A complete system for crafting presentations.

- *Connect through Emotional Intelligence*: Systems for increasing your EI—which is more important than your IQ.

- *Speak and Meet Virtually*: Systems for becoming a "Zoom rock star," including effectively leading and participating in meetings.

In the next few chapters, I'm going to give you systems aimed at the three areas that have been the biggest confidence-killers for my clients: developing a prepared talk (a highly abbreviated version of *Write to Speak*), off-the-cuff speaking, and avoiding rambling while speaking. Clearly, these aren't the only systems you'll ever need, but they'll go a long way toward helping you craft a confident message.

CHAPTER 11

Standard Speech System

There are many kinds of speeches, but as the title "standard speech system" indicates, I'm not being overly specific here. For the purposes of this chapter, a speech is defined as any sort of spoken presentation, toast, message, sermon, or lecture that has been prepared in advance. This system is very flexible and can be used in many different settings. With some practice, you should be able to adapt it to your specific needs.

Because it is the first system, we'll take a little longer with it, but this discussion is still very brief. If you want a more complete treatment, please see my book *Write to Speak*, from which this chapter is adapted.[1]

GETTING STARTED

Julia Andrews, playing Maria in *The Sound of Music*, said—sang, actually—that the beginning is a very good place to start. While that may be true of learning musical notes (though I never personally learned them), it's not true of writing a speech. The beginning is pretty much the very worst place to start. Why? Two reasons:

- First, you can't really write the introduction until you know what you're going to say in the rest of the speech. The introduction is actually the last part you'll write in this system.

- Second, the beginning is also the *hardest* part to write. You'll experience the pressure to find the perfect opening sentence and struggle to settle on the right first word. Before you know it, you're paralyzed with second guesses and bingeing *Game of Thrones* sounds much better than writing. It's better to start with something that builds momentum, not stops it. However, if some burst of inspiration for the intro hits you, you should write it and keep going as long as it flows. Stop when it stops and go back to what you were doing.

So, if you're not supposed to start at the beginning, where should you start? Read on for the six steps of the standard speech system.

1. Start with the Questions

The questions are:

- **Why** am I giving this speech? Why do I care?
- **What** is the purpose of the speech?
- **Who** is the audience?
- **Why** should *they* care?
- **What** is the point?

Do those sound familiar? If you're old enough or know your classic movies, you should be hearing Mr. Miyagi saying, "Wax on, wax off" right about now. (And if you have no idea what I'm talking about, you need to watch *Karate Kid*, vintage 1984, which is the source material for *Cobra Kai* on Netflix.) The point is that all the lessons you've learned in this section have intentionally led to this. If you did your work in Chapters 8 and 9, you've basically completed this first step.

a. Why Am I Giving This Speech? Why Do I Care?

On the top of the first page of your speech, write "I am giving this speech because ____." This question brings your speech back to your identity—because *you* are the message (Chapter 2). Don't settle on surface answers like, "My boss told me to" or "It's my duty as the maid of honor." Instead, dig deeper and connect it to your mission and values (Chapter 4), such as communicating something you believe in, honoring your best friend, or providing clarity to your colleagues.

The goal of this question is to ground your speech in something you care about because you'll be confident in what you care about. Conviction amplifies confidence.

Conviction amplifies confidence.

So, if I were preparing a speech on using systems for speech writing, I might write, "My mission is to help people realize their potential. I believe this tool can help them reach new heights."

b. What Is the Purpose of the Speech?

Next, write, "The purpose of my speech is to____." Use action words—like *persuade, inform, motivate*—followed by the content. So, it may read, "The purpose of my speech is to convince my listeners to use my systems for writing their speeches."

The verb you choose will be driven by what kind of speech you are giving. Here are the four broad categories and some of the action words you could use with each:

- Informative speech: Inform, show, demonstrate, prove, or educate.

- Persuasive speech: Persuade, prove, motivate, convince, sell, or pitch.

- Entertainment speech: Entertain, make laugh, or lighten moods.

- Special event speech: Honor, eulogize, celebrate, or connect.

Try to make this purpose statement as brief, clear, and specific as possible. The longer, vaguer, and more confusing it is, the less effective it will be.

c. Who Are the Audience?

Under the purpose, write, "My audience will be_____." You don't need to write a multipage profile, just enough to summarize the research you did from Chapter 9. So, I might write, "My audience will be middle-management professionals who are intimidated by writing speeches."

d. Why Should They Care?

Write, "The reason they care is____." Do not skip this step. It's the key to an eager audience and keeps you focused on serving them. This in turn increases confidence in your message. So, I could write, "The reason they care is because great public speaking skills make them more valuable and can enhance their earning potential."

e. What Is the Point?

Finally, write, "The point of my speech is____." As I said in Chapter 8 and 9, the point should tie the speech's purpose with the audience's reason for caring and be expressed as the singular thing you want them to know/do. So, I might write, "The point of my speech is that, by using my system, my audience can write better speeches in less time, increasing their confidence and effectiveness."

(Note: You can download a template of these questions at connect.mikeacker.com.)

2. Brainstorm Using a "Mind Map"

A mind map is simply a diagram used for the purpose of visually organizing information. It's been around for a while, but I've found it works especially well as a brainstorming tool. Because it is a tool, you shouldn't feel chained to a specific method, but start with this one and then figure out what works best for you.

Mind mapping is primarily a brainstorming session, and the most important principle of brainstorming is no filter. Write whatever comes to your mind without editing—yet. In his presentation on creativity, Monty Python's John Cleese talked about the two modes of thinking and their respective value:

> We all operate in two contrasting modes, which might be called open and closed. The open mode is more relaxed, more receptive, more exploratory, more democratic, more playful, and more humorous.
>
> The closed mode is the tighter, more rigid, more hierarchical, more tunnel-visioned. Most people, unfortunately, spend most of their time in the closed mode. Not that the closed mode cannot be helpful.
>
> If you are leaping a ravine, the moment of takeoff is a bad time for considering alternative strategies. When you charge the enemy machine-gun post, don't waste energy trying to see the funny side of it. Do it in the "closed" mode.
>
> But the moment the action is over, try to return to the "open" mode—to open your mind again to all the feedback from our action that enables us to tell whether the action has been successful or whether further action is needed to improve on what we have done. In other words, we must return to the open mode because in

that mode we are the most aware, most receptive, most creative, and therefore at our most intelligent.[2]

His point throughout the presentation is that open and closed thinking are necessary at certain times. Create in open. Evaluate the creation in closed. Brainstorming must be done in open mode—stream of consciousness, quantity over quality, there is no such thing as a bad idea, and so forth. You need to get into an almost playful mindset to brainstorm well. Yes, this even applies to more serious topics, such as quarterly reviews, board presentations, and memorials. It can open your mind to unexpected insights.

When brainstorming, I use a mind map to both gather and guide my work. A mind map can be created electronically, using a computer or tablet, or by using a physical medium (such as paper or sticky notes on a board). Both have their advantages and disadvantages. The electronic form is easier to save, edit, and share but is more prone to distractions (such as technical difficulties and having easy access to the internet). The simplicity of paper and the tactile nature of handwriting allow creativity to flow, but it's easily lost and harder to edit. Experiment with each and see which works best for you.

Begin by writing the one- to two-word version of your point in the middle of the page.

Now, brainstorm any material you might want to share about your topic. Here are some questions to get you started. The purpose of your speech may affect which questions are more relevant, but don't try to guide your brainstorming (remember, you're in open mode now):

- What do my listeners need to know about my topic?
- Why do I care about it? What is my personal history with it?
- What sort of things do I tend to say about my topic in casual conversations?
- What proof or evidence do I have?
- What are some common objections?
- What are some supporting materials—statistics, examples, stories, analogies, etc.—I can use?
- What are some parallel ideas to my topic?
- What have others said about it?
- How has my topic shown up in the business world or popular culture?

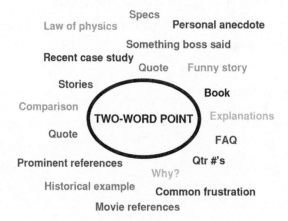

Notice that I didn't use full sentences or complete thoughts. You only need enough to remember what you meant. As you brainstorm, you might see some sort of order develop. Maybe certain ideas easily lend themselves to ones already on the page, so you cluster them around each other. This is where the sticky note method can be advantageous.

Ideally, you shouldn't do all your brainstorming in one session. Your brain will keep working in the background even when you walk away. It's not uncommon to get your best material in the second session—or even when you're doing something completely unrelated.

When are you done? The short answer is when you have a good deal more material than you'll need. Think of it this way: Imagine that you're building a tree fort in your backyard. The cost of the materials is no issue, but the hardware store is two hours from the house. If at all possible, you want to get all of your supplies in one trip, so you get extra of everything. Better too many nails than a trip back to the hardware store. At the same time, you wouldn't want to go crazy because you'll have to sort and carry everything you buy. You'll basically keep your purchases proportional to the size of the tree house you have planned. That is to say, the longer and more complex the topic, the more material you'll need.

3. Organize Your Points

Once you're satisfied with your material, you'll need to shift from open to closed mode. It's time to evaluate, categorize, and organize everything you did in the last step. First, a general word about the structure of speeches. The specifics will be driven by the purpose of your speech, but every speech consist of three parts:

The **introduction** functions the same as the introduction of a book. Its one purpose is to hook the audience and keep them listening. An introduction shouldn't offer any complete ideas but only make promises about what the body will provide.

The **body** contains all the actual content of the speech and does the heavy lifting.

The **conclusion** should not contain any new information. Its purpose is to summarize what has been said and tell the listener what to do/feel/think next.

The introduction and conclusion each get their own steps, so we're not going to worry about them too much now other than setting aside any brainstorming material that seems useful. Because the body is longer and more complex than the other parts, it can seem more intimidating. But it only has to be as difficult as you make it.

If you're a student of design, you've heard of things like the golden ratio, the rule of thirds, the Fibonacci Sequence, and the principle of symmetry. There are some arrangements that are more naturally pleasing to the human eye and mind. The number three holds the same power in communication. For whatever reason, we are naturally inclined to express and—more importantly—remember things in groups of three. One example is the adage that "bad things come in three." It's not at all true, but we naturally group events in threes (especially in the Western world). The point is you can use this inclination to your advantage by sticking with the three-point speech.

Humans are naturally inclined to express and remember things in groups of three.

Sometimes, my clients question my suggestion of three-point speeches. I can't blame them. I did the same for years. Three-point speeches seemed so *ordinary*. Over the years, I've experimented with all kinds of "more creative" speeches. Sometimes, they worked; more often they flopped, and they always took way more time and effort. Remember, your goal isn't to write the next Gettysburg Address. You just want a really good speech that will effectively communicate your main point with minimum hair-pulling.

Here's the painless way to organize your speech. Begin by going through all your material from the 10,000-foot view to get a sense of the overarching ideas. Look for the three most important ideas, which will become your three points. What if you can't narrow it down to three? Hang on to the extra ones for now, but keep looking for ways to combine them. You may not be able to—a speech about the six steps of the standard speech system will require six steps. But remember this: The more points a speech has, the less likely your audience will be able to remember them. As I said in Chapter 7, you can't change how much listeners is able to retain, but you can change the likelihood of them remembering the things you want them to.

The more points a speech has, the less likely your audience will be able to remember them.

So, now, you (ideally) have three highly focused points, which I call "buckets." They are the containers that will hold all the speech's key information. They literally give the audience a place to put everything they hear, so they can carry it away with them. Hence, buckets.

Here's how buckets aid remembrance. If you were to ask me what toys my son likes to play with (which would be kind of weird, but let's go with it), I could pull fifty toys off his shelf and announce them one by one. How many of the fifty do you think you'd remember an hour later? Maybe the first couple and the last one (because you were so relieved it was the last) and maybe a few in the middle.

Let's say I understand the power of buckets, so instead I grab about a dozen toys and items and sort them into the three buckets: action figures, Hot Wheels, and DJ equipment (yes, my six-year-old son likes to DJ—he offers a special rate for birthday parties, if you're interested) and then talk about each bucket. An hour later, you might still remember all twelve objects. You would've seen fewer of his toys than with the no-bucket approach but would remember more (that's key—less is more), and you'd have a far better understanding of my son's play habits.

So, once you have chosen your three buckets, go through all your material again, this time examining each piece and placing them in one of six categories:

1. Introduction: Material that elicits interest, presents problems that need to be solved, makes promises about the body, etc.

2. Bucket 1

3. Bucket 2

4. Bucket 3

5. Conclusion: Material that summarizes the buckets and presents next steps.

6. Unsorted: Perhaps the most useful category because it's easier to *set aside* the one great idea that doesn't really fit than it is to toss it.

This is where the sticky note method is nice—you can physically move them around and try different arrangements. Does the story about the python in your basement go better with Bucket 1 or Bucket 2? Just move it back and forth, and see what feels better.

Once you have sorted all your brainstorming material into one of these categories (and tossed any that didn't make the cut), step away for a while, allowing yourself to return to open mode. Go do something fun, work on a different project, exercise, sleep on it. Your brain will keep working.

When you return, take a fresh look at your categories and the material in them. Does Bucket 1 need less content? Should more material be sent to "Unsorted"? If you have more than three buckets, can any of them be combined or eliminated?

Now, it's time to examine your buckets individually. As I've already indicated, you must be absolutely clear about the central idea of each point. If it isn't clear in your head, it won't be clear to your audience.

If it isn't clear in your head, it won't be clear to your audience.

One of the best tools for focusing your points is naming them, that is, creating titles. A great title will practically write the point. My fourth book began with nothing more than the idea for a title, *Lead with No Fear*. These titles can describe the content of buckets, present actions to be taken, be pithy one-liners, or be chronologically or process-driven (i.e. Step 1, Step 2, Step 3). When it comes to titles, clarity is better than cleverness. It doesn't matter how creative it is if the audience doesn't understand it. If nothing else, start by writing a summary of the point, and then keep editing it down into the minimum number of words possible. If you can get it down to three or four words, you'll have an effective title. More importantly, you'll have personal clarity.

After you know the point of each bucket, look at all three and how they relate to each other and—most importantly—how they relate to the overarching point and purpose of the speech. Do the buckets flow from one to the next? Do they work together to accomplish your speech's purpose? A great point that distracts from the main point is not a good point.

A great point that distracts from the main point is not a good point.

Does this feel like a lot of work? It's a lot less work to find these problems now rather than in the final draft. And it's even worse to realize, halfway through giving your presentation, that one point is completely irrelevant. Believe me.

Once you know the point of each bucket, you'll be able to sort through material in each with one simple question: Does this explain or support my point? If not, toss it. If you can't bear getting rid of it, move it to Unsorted. Now, you can organize the remaining material within each bucket. Here are some possible structures: (Note: Some of these are also useful for organizing your buckets within the larger speech.)

- Problem/Solution/Testimony
- Problem/False solution/True solution
- Theory/Evidence/Action
- Concept/Explanation
- Mystery/Answer
- Idea/Illustration
- Strengths/Weaknesses/Opportunities & Threats
- Past/Present/Future
- Finances/Operations/Personnel
- Need/Product/The Ask

Play with these ideas, and see what fits your situation the best but always remember to stay focused on the point of the bucket. How will each thing you say enforce the point? By the way, this is one of the great strengths of the bucket system. When (not if) you realize mid-speech that you forget to say something, it won't really matter. So long as they remember the bucket, it's a win.

Once you're comfortable with your speech's organization, put it on pause and move on to the next step. We'll refine it in step six, giving your subconscious more time to work on it.

4. Write the Conclusion

I call this landing the plane. Done right, your conclusion will summarize your key points, give your audience clear direction for their next steps, and motivate them to go out and do it. Done wrong, it will undo everything you did right in the rest of the speech. No one cares how good the flight was if the plane crashes on landing. A good conclusion has (can you guess?) three components:

a. The Summary

Finish your last point, pause to signal a transition, recap the three points (without adding any new information!), then give a well-crafted "this is the big idea" statement.

b. The Outcome

Present the desired outcome from your speech. What are the audience's next steps? This could be for them to

- . . . know something (educational presentations, lectures, lessons, etc.),
- . . . do something (motivational speeches, action-oriented sermons, instruction), or
- . . . feel something (toasts, ceremonies, inspirational speeches).

c. The Closing

Finish your speech strong, with one or two well-crafted sentences that are delivered confidently and with purpose. When you are done, you are done. Don't ruin a perfect landing by adding another mini-flight.

5. Write the Introduction

As I said at the beginning of this chapter, the introduction is the single most important part of the speech. It is your one opportunity to convince your audience to entrust you with their time and attention. In my experience, you have this much time:

- Eight seconds to give a good first impression.
- Two minutes to capture attention.
- Five minutes to give them a reason to listen to the body.

These are the three phases of the opening, each leading to the next, with the single purpose of preparing your audience to listen to the body of the speech with the highest level of receptivity.

a. First Impression

Eight seconds is roughly the time it takes to walk to the front and say your first sentence (or for you to say your first words coming off of mute on Zoom). By that point, your audience will have already made an initial judgment about you, which is driven primarily by whatever they discern about your identity (another reason we spent so much time on that). Audiences can sense if someone is insecure, disingenuous, or self-serving. If you're speaking to people who already know you, they'll already have an impression of you, making your first sentence even more crucial for setting the tone.

That to say, your first sentence is a precious commodity, so don't waste it on things like introducing yourself or thanking the emcee: These can be woven into a later part of the speech. Instead, craft a powerful hook, and let that be the first words they hear from you. How do you create a great hook? Read on.

b. Capture Attention

We talk about the honeymoon period to describe the time in any new partnership—a marriage, a new CEO, a new employee—when everyone gives each other the benefit of the doubt. Every speech or presentation is a type of partnership. The audience and speaker are working together for the imparting of ideas, and the audience will typically give you no more than two minutes to demonstrate that you'll live up to your end of the bargain.

The goal in this phase is to hook your audience and create interest by reeling them into the next phase, cementing their impression of you, and laying the foundation for the body of the speech. That last part is crucial. Too many speakers waste their first impression with an irrelevant anecdote. This wastes time and erodes trust.

For that reason, it's vital not to waste time with throat-clearing—a writing term for unproductive words. Instead, jump right into a killer hook. I've discovered that there are five primary hooks, each of which can be used in one of three different "modes," yielding fifteen different high-impact ways to capture attention. The three modes are:

1. **Being Relatable**
   This says, "I'm like you, and my material is relevant to you" and is especially valuable when there is an apparent distance (such as age or education) between you and the audience that you want to bridge.

2. **Being Funny**

This says, "I'm likable, and my material is interesting" and is especially valuable when you want your audience to drop their guard and entertain your ideas.

3. **Being Unexpected**

This says, "I'm an interesting person, and my material will engage you" and is especially valuable when your audience (1) has low expectations of you or your speech or (2) is already on information overload, such as at a trade conference.

As you read through the following five hooks, think about how each of them can be used in a relatable, funny, or unexpected mode.

1. **Question:** Starting immediately with a question or series of questions will force the listeners to mentally engage with you.

2. **Quote:** A strong opening quote can invoke the authority of another while holding it at a distance from yourself.

3. **Statement:** A well-crafted opening statement is like a quote except that it comes from the speaker. This may lessen its authority but shows you're taking full responsibility for the idea.

4. **Statistic:** Used well (and sparingly), statistics can quickly and authoritatively convey a need.

5. **Story:** Stories can be the most labor-intensive to craft but are also the most effective for bypassing the head and going straight for the heart.

Were you able to think of how each hook could be used in each mode? Test yourself by going to an exercise at connect. mikeacker.com and connecting the fifteen opening sentences with their hook/mode.

As you craft the introduction, take note that the connection between your hook and point doesn't need to be immediately apparent. We've all heard great speeches where we didn't fully understand the opening until the conclusion.

c. Reason to Listen

The final phase of the introduction is to give your audience a reason to listen. The good news is that you already have this, assuming you "started with the questions" (step one of the system). The fourth question was "Why should they care?" All you are doing in this phase is answering this.

Carnegie called it arousing an eager want. I describe it as "painting the pain." Your job is to make your audience realize how badly they want something and then promising to give it to them. Of course, the term "pain" is relative. If you're giving a wedding toast, the pain may be no more than teasing them with the promise of a really embarrassing story about the groom. In any case, if your introduction can promise a solution to well-painted pain, you'll have fully engaged audience. But don't deliver the solution (yet). Like any good cliffhanger, you want to leave them dangling for a little while.

> **If your introduction can promise (but not yet deliver) a solution to well-painted pain, you'll have a fully engaged audience.**

6. Edit for Flow

The final step, editing, is the easiest in some ways and the hardest in others. It's the easiest because the uncertainty has been removed. The pieces are in place; now all that is left is grunt work. It's the hardest because now it's time to start reading out loud, which you've probably been avoiding. But I can't overemphasize how important this is. Things that look wonderful on paper just don't work the same when spoken. This is the step where you transform the vision in your head into reality. I like to read through my speeches in three separate stages.

a. Read and Reinforce

In the first read-through, ask, "What's missing?" Don't worry about transitions between ideas; that happens in the next stage. Here you're asking if you've said everything you need to say. Are your points clear? Do they need more illustrations or evidence? The more thorough your mind mapping was, the less work you'll have here.

b. Read and Revise

Get more critical in this read-through. Examine each point and ask if there's a better way to say it. Always look for ways to make it clearer and shorter. Make sure everything flows in a logical order, and experiment with moving pieces around.

This is the time to examine your transitions. Does each item flow naturally from one to the next? Utilize the KISS (Keep It Simple, Stupid) principle here and don't make transitions any more complicated than necessary. Sometimes they can be as simple as a pause (between sub-points) or a one-sentence summary of a main point.

c. Read and Refine

This is the fine-tuning read-through. Look for any rough edges, anything that catches you as you speak it out loud. Better to fix it now than stumble mid-speech. This stage can be particularly painful because, 95% of the time, you'll have to cut material. The question is not "Is everything here good?" but "Does everything contribute *uniquely* to the point I want to make?" If you have two great stories that basically say the same thing, keep the better of the two.

If you haven't already timed your speech, do so now. If you tend to talk fast and stick to your notes, assume your speech will go shorter than you think. If you tend to expand on your outline or ramble, assume it will go longer. The results may mean you need to add or subtract more material.

When are you done editing? When you feel that (1) the main point is clear and the speech accomplishes its purpose, (2) no crucial material is missing, and (3) you can give it to yourself in a mirror comfortably. Don't stop until all those are in place.

7. (Optional) Create a Visual Presentation

If your speech calls for a visual presentation (such as PowerPoint, Slide Deck, etc.), treat it as a part of the speech, not an afterthought and not as the first act. Speak through your visual presentation, not around it. I cover this more in *Speak and Meet Virtually*, but you want to make sure that your presentation enhances your message and doesn't distract from it. I've also discovered that creating the presentation often improves my speech. Writing a slide with a main point, for instance, forces me to refine its wording.

Speak through your visual presentation, not around it.

———

As I said at the beginning, this is the standard speech system and is the foundation for all the other ones. In the next chapter, we'll explore systems for speaking when you are unable to prepare.

CHAPTER 12

Spontaneous Speech System

You don't always have the luxury of preparing your speech. Spontaneous speaking, that is, speaking without notes or preparation, is something most of us face on a regular basis. Examples include impromptu speeches, Q & A sessions, meetings, interviews, or simply being put on the spot. Some people seem natural and prefer it to prepared speeches. For them, pressure spurs greater creativity and clarity. For others, it paralyzes them and crushes their confidence. If that's you, then you're going to love this chapter. Over the years, I've developed systems aimed at building your confidence even when the pressure is on. The good news is they build off everything you've learned already.

In the previous chapter, I mentioned, "Wax on, wax off," from *Karate Kid*. In an iconic scene, Daniel-san thinks that Mr. Miyagi has been using him as free labor when in fact he's been training his muscles to perform certain defensive moves. This alludes to karate's uses of "katas," carefully prescribed patterns of movements and stances that are practiced continually. Students of karate spend more time practicing katas than fighting. It's not that *senseis* (teachers) think someone will attack you in that exact pattern. It's all about muscle memory—teaching your body how to respond without thinking. Martial arts aren't a mystical endowment of superhuman speed and strength but a deliberate training of things like stance, breathing, and muscle memory. The work done in advance prepares you for moments you can't prepare for.

The work done in advance prepares you for moments you can't prepare for.

The most important part of preparation for spontaneous speaking comes from (you guessed it) your identity. Think of this being like your stance in karate. A person who understands their center of balance and knows how to stand can topple a person twice their size that is not well-grounded. In the same way, if you know who you are and don't need your audience's approval to be grounded, you can go into speaking situations without the demoralizing fear of failure. Perhaps, as you've worked on your identity, you've already noticed that your confidence is increasing without even "trying."

The second part of the preparation comes from the systems I'm going to teach you. Think of them like the katas, but instead of muscle memory, these build mental memory and are specific habits and tools that will teach you to react quicker and more effectively.

Let's first think about the way we usually respond to a question we're not prepared to answer. I call it the shotgun approach. Or we could call it verbal vomit, but that's not as polite. Basically, we say whatever comes to mind in whatever order it comes. But our minds can be like my son's room after his friends come over. Open books laying all round, clothes in a pile by his dresser, DJ equipment on his bed, DC action figures and Transformers locked in battle on the floor, and a minefield of Legos wanting to be discovered by my bare feet. When I tell him there's no dinner until he has picked up, he's tempted to shove as much of the mess into a single large, overflowing bucket.

The shotgun approach is the verbal equivalent of dumping that large bucket into your listeners' lap. You've technically answered the question (and then some), but it wasn't what they were looking for, and you're not very proud of the results. Afterward, you'll think about all the things you meant to say but forgot. Even worse are the things you wish you hadn't said. People have been fired for things said during a nervous ramble.

We use this same approach to cover our lack of preparation. It was my "trick" throughout high school. When it came to essay questions on exams, I couldn't target the exact answer, so I just wrote as much as I could (like a spray of pellets in a shotgun), hoping that something would hit the target. This may work on some people but will cost you credibility with more intelligent and better-informed listeners.

The trick to better spontaneous speaking is buying yourself a little extra in-the-moment preparation time in order to better leverage your beforehand preparation, that is, what you already know about the topic. These systems aren't substitutes for knowing your stuff—this isn't a course on BS-ing your way through. They help you unlock what you know.

Spontaneous speaking systems aren't a substitute for knowing your stuff.

1. THE SPELLING BEE SYSTEM

Like many of you, spelling bees were a part of my elementary years. In these events, students stand in front of a panel of judges and spells a word on the spot. Students can't sound it out or ask for a redo. However, there are some tools available to them. After contestants is asked to spell a word, they are allowed to ask for the word to be repeated, for its definition, and to hear it used in a sentence.

Most spontaneous speaking starts with some kind of question, similar to being given a word to spell, but you need to understand that you don't have to answer immediately. That's the key. You're "allowed" to do a couple things first, starting with asking for the question to be repeated. Even saying, "I'm sorry, would you please repeat that?" buys you time to think. Those couple extra seconds may make the difference between clarity and a muddled answer.

Next, contestants are allowed to ask for clarification—a definition and to hear it used in a sentence. This is crucial because a lot of words sound similar, and fine distinctions are easily missed when the entire school's eyes are on you. "Elocution," for instance, sounds a lot like "electrocution." Without clarification, the contestant could easily end up spelling the wrong word.

The same is true when you are put on the spot. The adrenaline running through your body makes you action-prone and susceptible to misunderstandings. By simply asking for clarification, you can ensure you're answering the right question. Otherwise, you could end up spending a long time on a rabbit trail. Or maybe you've been asked a very broad question, like "What's the fourth quarter looking like for the company?" That's a big question with many possible answers, so you could respond, "Are you asking about marketing? Product development? Or overall revenue?" Not only have you bought yourself more time and ensured that you answer the right question, but you've also utilized two other effective strategies.

- First, your brain is a very powerful processor. The information is in there (assuming you've done your homework); you just need to prime the pump. The very act of asking the clarifying question has started the processing. Even as you suggested possible topics—marketing, product development, revenue—responses to each category began to form.

- Second, you've switched from defense to offense, from being put on the spot to engaging the other person. This can be incredibly empowering and can even raise your credibility while demonstrating that you were listening and are taking the question seriously.

There are still four more systems for spontaneous speech, but I started with this one because it can be used as the starting point for any of the other ones.

2. The Sniper System

I said earlier that I used the shotgun approach on essay questions in high school. My sister used the sniper system: She put all her power into a single response delivered with precision and clarity. This demonstrated tremendous confidence in her answer. There was no barrage of words to hide any weak-thinking; either she knew the answer or she didn't. And she usually did.

Here's an important dynamic to understand: When we're talking, we feel like more words equal more authority. When we're listening, we think the opposite. The more you say, the less people believe it.

The more you say, the less people believe it.

There's another dynamic to pay attention to. In interviews and Q & As, we often feel each question requires an answer of similar length. It may even feel disrespectful to give a short answer. But some questions just don't require more. If you asked me my son's age, I could respond, "Well, he just turned six, on Sunday actually. But we had our family birthday party on Friday. It was a lot of fun. On Sunday, we had a big birthday party. It was Mario themed . . . ." Or I could say, "He just turned six." The point is that we stress ourselves out by expecting to provide more of an answer than they asked for or even wanted.

The sniper system aims for maximum impact and clarity with a minimum of words. The way it works is simple. Pause for a moment, maybe ask a clarifying question, then answer the question succinctly. When you're done, you may even end with, "Is there anything you'd like me to add?" Not because you doubt your "sniper shot" but as an offer to hit a few more targets. That question can be helpful for three additional reasons. First, it makes it easier for you to finish because you're giving them an opportunity to ask for more information if you didn't say enough. Second, it ends your answer with finality and forces you to stop. It's usually what we say *after* we've answered the question that we end up regretting. Finally, it puts the ball back in their court and neutralizes the "silence tactic." You know what I mean—how interviewers and negotiators try to get more out of you by letting you fill the silence.

The sniper system aims for maximum impact and clarity with minimum words.

This system is especially useful in job interviews, particularly the dreaded, "What is your greatest weakness?" question. To that you could answer, "I'm not detail-oriented, so I need to surround myself with a quality team. Would you like me to elaborate?"

3. THE "ONCE UPON A TIME" SYSTEM

Steven Spielberg's critically acclaimed movie, *Lincoln* (based on the biography *Team of Rivals* by Doris Kearns Goodwin), accurately portrays Abraham Lincoln's habit of constant storytelling. Some of his cabinet, including Secretary of War Edwin Stanton, thought it a foolish waste of time, but the viewer can see Lincoln's strategy. He used the stories to move hearts, communicate essential information, and moderate the mood of a room.

Stories are powerful. Done well, a story, illustration, or a fable can convey far more—and on more levels—than simple facts. However, they can be challenging to pull off spontaneously. As with all the systems, prior preparation is the key here. If you're already in the habit of reading stories and using them in prepared speeches, they will come more readily. Furthermore, storytelling is a skill to be developed. When you tell a story to friends, do they stay engaged, or do their eyes wander? If you can't keep your friends' attention, then you're probably not yet ready to use storytelling in spontaneous speeches. Study the craft of storytelling and practice with friends.

Here's how to use this system. As with the previous ones, buy some time and quickly ask yourself two questions. First, *What is the point I want to convey?* And second, *Have I experienced anything or know a story that relates to that point?* You don't need to have it all mapped out in your head before starting; just keep your point in mind as you tell the story. Your subconscious will work on connecting the story with your point. Worst-case scenario: End the story and say, "I forgot where I was going with that!" and then answer the question in a different way. If you can laugh at yourself, then everyone else will truly laugh *with*, not at, you.

4. THE THREE BUCKET SYSTEM

You've already met the three buckets in the standard speech system, but they are even more powerful in this spontaneous speech system. Think again of the story about my son's messy room at the beginning of this chapter. What if, instead of telling him to pick up his room, I gave him three baskets, one for clothes, one for toys, and one for everything else? The results will be far more organized than with the single basket.

Here is a principle I've already hinted at: Your mouth mobilizes your mind. If you begin your answer with the words, "I have three thoughts about that . . . ." you are effectively telling your brain to go clean up its room and handing it three empty buckets. Have faith in your brain—you don't need to have chosen all three points, only the first bucket. Start talking about that one, and your brain will start sorting everything. As you finish the first bucket, you'll find the second one ready to go, and the third one after that.

Your mouth mobilizes your mind.

Another crucial point: Just as with the three buckets in the previous chapter, you don't need to say every possible thing about each bucket. You simply need to ensure that each point gets across. Again, people don't need the perfect answer, just a good one. Don't belabor any bucket (more words = less authority), and end your answer with a brief summary of all three.

5. THE STICKY NOTE SYSTEM

I was recently being interviewed for a podcast that reaches 22,000 people, and about halfway through the interview, the host asked me a question that was off the topic and fairly controversial. There are times when you'll be put on the spot, and a misstep can have significant ramifications. That's when this system can be a lifesaver as it was for me that day.

I said to the host, "Wow, that is a really important question, and I want to make sure I respond well. Can you give me a couple seconds to gather my thoughts?"

Of course, he couldn't say no, and I used that time to write my three buckets on a sticky note in the form of three words. That took maybe three seconds, so I added a couple more words to the buckets, and then I looked up and answered with a response I'm still proud of.

Whereas the Spelling Bee system tries to buy time, this one flat out asks for it. It seems so obvious, but we rarely do it. Why not? Because we believe it looks bad not to have an immediate response. But it doesn't. Watch a Jordan Peterson interview. He has no problem making us wait while he thinks through an answer, and regardless of your opinion of him, no one can accuse him of being stupid. His delay demonstrates his thoughtfulness. And consider, which will make you look worse: asking for five to ten seconds or stammering and using filler words for twenty seconds while you gather your thoughts?

A caveat: Don't overuse this system. Asking for time to answer a question that you should have at the top of your head *will* make you look unprepared or lacking in confidence. Save it for the really big deal questions that require extra thought.

Here's how to use this system. When asked a complicated question or one that is potentially hazardous to your career, acknowledge the question (getting clarification, if needed) and ask for ten seconds to gather your thoughts, then jot down the top three things you want to say (on a sticky note, the margins of a book, or in your phone's notepad). You'll be surprised by how little time this will take. This is an exercise I do with my clients, and they always come up with three buckets for any question. You can accomplish more in ten seconds of silence than in thirty seconds while you're talking.

Once you have three words/buckets, quickly determine how much time to spend on each. This is crucial because we tend to spend more time on our first point, regardless of its relative importance, stealing valuable time (and audience attention span) from the rest. That done, thank the interviewer for the time and answer the question. End by briefly summarizing your three points and asking if there is anything they want you to add.

PRACTICE SYSTEMS, NOT SPONTANEITY

I want you to shift your mindset. Don't call it spontaneous speaking; say *systems speaking* instead. At the beginning of this chapter, I compared the systems to katas in karate. By practicing these forms in advance, you can prepare yourself to respond better in the moment. It isn't about being more spontaneous but more practiced.

It isn't about being more spontaneous but more practiced.

One great exercise for speaking off the cuff is what I call expository reading. Find a book from your industry and randomly choose a paragraph. Read a couple of sentences out loud and then comment (exposit) on them. Time yourself and go for as long as you can. Choose a different passage and try to go for longer. It's vital that you do this out loud. Better yet, in front of a mirror or on a recording. As you improve, do it in front of friends.

Another great practice is role playing. Have someone play the part of the angry customer, the nice customer, and the obtuse customer.

You can also practice with a coworker by asking each other questions that apply to your industry. Intentionally use a different system with each question. You're practicing off stage what you want to happen on stage.

- Ask them to repeat the question.
- Ask a clarifying question.
- Answer a question with as few words as possible.
- Answer with a story or illustration.
- Began an answer with, "I have three thoughts about that . . . ." before you know the three points.
- Ask for ten seconds to think about your answer, and jot down three points and prioritize them.

Continuing with the sticky note system, try listening to podcasts and interviews on various topics, and when a challenging question is asked, turn off the volume and practice writing your three points.

Another great way to practice, especially if you're going to be interviewed soon, is to collect as many potential questions as possible and then asking and answering them out loud and in front of a mirror. This kind of practice will help you even with questions that didn't make your list.

At the beginning, I mentioned how some people seem naturally comfortable when they're put on the spot. Likewise, Bruce Lee or Jackie Chan make martial arts *look* natural, but we know it takes much more than talent. It takes years and years of practice. This is true of speaking as well. The "naturals" simply learned their systems early on and have been practicing as a natural part of their life. With time and intentionality, you too can find confidence through spontaneous systems.

Rambling. We all do it, using more words than we need and repeating ourselves again and again and going off on irrelevant tangents, like the time I rode my long board down a steep, busy highway. I hit a rock, and I went flying and . . . never mind. The point is, we all need to stop rambling, and in the next chapter, I give you a five-point system just for that.

CHAPTER 13

Rambling-Reduction Systems

In *Speak with No Fear*, I talk about an announcement for a service project that I gave to my university's student body. Nerves completely took over, and my short speech turned into senseless rambling. I was saying nothing and using a lot of words to do it. The president gently interrupted me and thanked me for sharing, then briefly summarized the key information. Thanks to him, the turnout was better than it should have been, but my confidence took a hit, and it was a while until I wanted to speak in front of a group again.

Everyone rambles. Sometimes, it's caused by nerves as happened to me. Sometimes, it's a lack of planning. Sometimes, it's because we feel we have so much to say. And sometimes, it's because we like hearing ourselves speak. Whatever the cause, a rambling speech is not a confident speech. Even if the speaker feels confident, rambling does not sound or appear that way. It creates an image that's the opposite of what you want.

A rambling speech is not a confident speech.

Many people treat rambling as a personal quirk instead of the serious issue that it is. That's why I'm building a case against it. Change is hard, and we'll seldom change unless we see a pressing need. At this point, some may try to defend it as a communication style. After all, what about Peter Falk's Columbo, a fictional character I grew up watching, who used rambling to solve every case? Yes, professional communicators can strategically use rambling in an effective way. Columbo used it to make himself appear incompetent and unsure of himself, allowing him to gather more clues because the suspects thought he was an idiot. That's probably not the look you're going for. At other times, a speaker might use rambling to momentarily distract while covertly building their main point. This is definitely an advanced skill. Best to leave rambling to the pros.

For the rest of us, think of it this way. When I'm hired for a company-wide training, that company has invested a lot of their resources to bring me in. They don't want me to waste ten minutes on pointless stories about my longboarding accidents. That's no better than a $500-an-hour lawyer wanting to hear all about your weekend. And it gets worse. Let's say there are fifty people in that training. If they earn an average of $100,000 a year, that equates to about $50 an hour. With fifty people in a meeting, that company is effectively paying me $41.60 per *minute* to ramble.

Have I made my case? It's time to address rambling habits and discover my two systems for doing so.

TYPES OF RAMBLING

For the sake of this chapter, rambling consists of any unplanned statements that do not move the speech forward (What about "planned statements"? Those are typically a case of poor speech writing, which we covered in Chapter 11.) Any given speech is going to move along a series of points, from A to Z. It doesn't necessarily need to take the straightest path. Hyperlinear speeches can be a little boring. But it must always move forward, toward the main point.

Rambling consists of statements, illustrations, and additional points that leave the path without a clear purpose. In my experience, there are basically four different types of rambling, each with its own unique causes.

1. Meandering

Meandering is when you're making your way through the speech, but then some fascinating idea catches your attention, leading you off on a rabbit trail until you've completely lost sight of the path and have to navigate back, often with words like, "Now, where was I? Oh, yeah. . . ."

Meandering may begin as a distraction or any semi-relevant idea, but it's enabled by the mistaken belief that everyone is interested in everything you say. It is essentially self-focused.

2. Circling Back

Circling back is where you've finished a point and start heading to the next, but then decide that you didn't hit that point well enough, so you circle back and hit it again. And again. And again.

Circling back is caused by a lack of trust—trust in yourself, your material, or your audience. It's driven by insecurity in your ability to communicate or theirs to understand you. Are there ever times to circle back? Sure. Experienced speakers are able to recognize when their listeners are confused and need to have a point clarified. *Experienced* speakers. Inexperienced speakers, however, are simply prone to doubt themselves. Here's a good rule of thumb: You have more clarity when you're writing a speech than when you're in the middle of giving it. It's best to continue on the path you planned rather than trying to create a new one on the spot.

> **You have more clarity when you're writing a speech than when you're giving it.**

3. Stuffing

Stuffing is a little different from standard rambling because you're following the outline and moving the speech forward, but you stuff each bucket with everything you know about the subject. It's usually extremely rushed or else drawn out but always boring.

$$A \text{-}\!\!\!\!\!\sim\!\!\!\!\!\!\text{-}Z$$

Stuffing may be driven by a lack of trust, just like circling back, but it frequently demonstrates a lack of training and understanding of the basic communication principle, "Less is more." The classic book on writing, *Elements of Style*, Rule 17 ("Omit needless words") says,

> Vigorous writing is concise. A sentence should contain no unnecessary words, a paragraph no unnecessary sentences, for the same reason that a drawing should have no unnecessary lines and a machine no unnecessary parts.

This requires not that the writer make all his sentences short, or that he avoid all detail and treat his subjects only in outline, but that every word tell.[1]

This is true of great writing and true of great speaking. It's bad enough that rambling wastes time and money, but it also squanders the audience's attention span—an even more limited resource. Said another way, rambling words displace more important words.

Rambling words displace more important words.

4. Verbal Processing

This is where you have a starting point and basically know where you're going, but you make it up—process it—as you go.

Verbal processing is basically a failure to prepare. To put it bluntly, it says your time is more valuable than the combined time of everyone listening. That, in fact, may be true. I worked for one gentleman who brought several of us in each week for a meeting that he seemed unprepared for. It took me a little while to realize he basically wanted us to listen to him verbally process. But he was in charge, and it was his budget, so that was his call. Verbal processing can be a very effective way to brainstorm, but it's a lousy way to give a speech or even lead a meeting. It's very disrespectful of your audience.

Rambling Reductions

Those are the four types of rambling, and there are two systems for reducing them, an immediate, "in the moment" system and a long-term one.

The immediate system consists of three simple steps: Notice, pause, and snap back.

1. Notice

As you speak, you'll eventually notice that you've left the path and are rambling about something that has nothing to do with anything. Or that you've returned to a previous point and are just repeating yourself. Or that you're shoving as much information into a bucket as possible. That is all you need to do at this step: Notice.

2. Pause

Once you've noticed that you're rambling, just pause. Let's say I'm giving a speech and suddenly notice that I'm talking about the time I was long boarding down a steep highway. All I should do is stop talking for a moment. It's easy to panic and react in a way that draws more attention to it. A pause gives you a chance to get back in control and resist the temptation to keep going. You might be afraid that you'll look bad if you don't continue, but depending on how long you've gone, your audience may not have fully realized that you're rambling (people usually aren't listening as closely as you think). And if they *have* realized it, they'll just be grateful you stopped. By simply pausing, you give yourself a moment to fix the problem with minimal distraction.

3. Snap Back

After you pause, just snap back. No apology, no fanfare. Just get back on the path. The less attention you give rambling, the less attention span you'll be stealing. It may feel unnatural to snap back without a transition such as, "Now, where was I" or "Let's get back to the main point," but it will feel far more natural to your audience. Perhaps they won't even notice what happened.

The less attention you give rambling, the less attention span you'll steal.

That's the immediate system, but the long-term solution will help you ramble less, notice it quicker, and snap back seamlessly.

1. Prepare Better

Think through your past presentations and examine which kind of rambling you're prone to and why you do it. Address the underlying issues:

- Is it a lack of trust in yourself and your material? Use the lessons of this book to improve your identity and message.

- Is it a lack of trust in the audience? Survey them afterward and see how well they understood.

- Is it believing everyone wants to hear your tangents? Find someone who will give honest feedback.

- Is it because of insufficient preparation? Prepare better next time.

2. Increase Awareness

Rambling can be so common that you don't even realize you're doing it. Listen to a recording of yourself. Better yet, use a transcription service, like Otter, to print off your speech and highlight all the places where you went off topic, repeated yourself, or stuffed a point too full. Ask someone you trust to evaluate your presentations for rambling. Consider working with a professional coach.

3. Practice "Failure"

Despite your best intentions, you will ramble. I teach this, and I still do it from time to time. Prepare yourself by intentionally "failing" and then noticing, pausing, and snapping back. My favorite way to do this is a variation of the expository reading technique from the last chapter. Grab a book and read a couple sentences (out loud!). When something catches your interest, start speaking spontaneously—rambling—about it. Allow yourself to get a little lost. Then notice, pause, and snap back, picking back up where you left off reading. Keep practicing this until "notice, pause, and snap back" becomes natural.

As I indicated at the end of Chapter 10, I've created systems for just about anything you can imagine. Now that you've seen several of mine, I hope you can create some of your own. Systems for presenting data, conducting employee evaluations, networking conversations that actually network—any speaking situation that you're frequently in. Just experiment with better ways of doing it, be okay with mistakes, make notes, and simplify it into a written system. I'd love to hear about any you create. Email me at info@stepstoadvance.com.

This wraps up the section on your messaging. Now, it's time to address the third source of confidence: developing your skills.

PART III

DEVELOP NEW SKILLS

CHAPTER 14

Increase Skills, Increase Confidence

When my nephew was younger, I'd hang out with him and be the cool uncle by showing him killer soccer moves. Growing up in Mexico, football wasn't really a thing, but "futbol" was, and I played at a competitive level throughout high school. Unfortunately, by the time he was a teenager—right after the Seahawk's first Superbowl win—all he cared about was football. Instead of soccer, he'd want to gear up and play a little football with me. Perhaps I could keep up with him as a six-year-old, but as the star wide receiver in high school, he could easily out-pass, out-rush, and out-tackle me. Being in my forties, the idea of a friendly "turkey bowl" game against him was enough for me to feign a knee injury. But get me out on the soccer field, and Uncle Mike can still teach those kids a thing or two.

Here's my point. When you increase your skills, you increase your confidence. I'm confident with soccer because I have some skills. Not MLS level, but enough to know what I'm doing. I lack confidence with football because I lack skills there.

In the Introduction, I distinguish between false confidence and true confidence. Alcohol is sometimes called "liquid courage" because it lowers inhibitions and makes you think you can do something, but that doesn't mean you actually can. This book isn't a shot of "speaking vodka"; we've been developing *true* confidence by focusing on each of its three sources: identity, message, and skills. Using the sailing analogy, I've said that identity is like the boat itself, message is the cargo, and skills are what it takes to handle the boat. Speaking with confidence requires all three. You may have the best boat in the world and be carrying precious cargo, but without sufficient sailing skills, you could still end up stranded on a reef.

HUMILITY AND CONFIDENCE

Imagine the skipper of an Alaskan crabbing boat who thinks nothing of going out into conditions that would terrify any sane person. He knows his boat, he knows his cargo, he knows his skills until he steps onto a three-masted schooner. It doesn't matter how well he knows his own boat; he's not going to feel confident on the schooner until he's picked up some new skills. His mastery of the crabbing boat could actually work *against* him if he's unwilling to let some college intern teach him how to work the schooner's sails.

I say this to remind all of us—myself included—that mastery in one area is not mastery in all. Without humility, we'll never be able to learn the necessary skills in a new area, and without those skills, we'll lack real confidence. It's easy to imagine that proud skipper experiencing insecurity on the schooner but hiding it behind a persona of confidence (Chapter 2).

Developing your confidence in speaking, therefore, requires humble awareness of when you need to develop a new set of skills. This awareness may come either from self-realization or someone else pointing it out—sometimes with the tact of a preschooler pointing out a "pregnant" person. Regardless of how the news is delivered, we've all had that sinking feeling of realizing that we aren't as good at something as we thought. What we do *after* that awareness is far more important than the awareness itself.

AWARENESS AND PRACTICE

Saint James once wrote that someone who hear the truth but doesn't do anything about it is like a person that looks into a mirror but then forget what they saw as soon as they walk away.[1] It's kind of a funny mental image—seeing a big piece of lettuce between your teeth but doing nothing about it. But ignoring it does not make it disappear; everyone else still sees the lettuce. You start with awareness, and then you move to practice. Without practice, awareness is worthless, but you can't practice until you know what needs to be fixed. Throughout the rest of this section, you'll see sections labeled "Awareness," "Practice," and "Awareness and Practice" that provide practical tools for you.

Without practice, awareness is worthless.

In Chapter 12, I compared systems to katas in karate and said that by developing "mental memory," you'll be able to respond the right way at the right time. The same is true of skills. They require practice. Just as you wouldn't walk down a dark alley right after learning your first kata, you shouldn't rush out on stage to try a new skill.

I have a friend who first learned to drive an automatic car and then bought one with a manual transmission. Initially, learning to drive stick shift made him feel like a worse driver. The same is true of new skills. At first, it may feel like you've gone backward, which is why I tell my clients again and again, "You need to practice offstage to perform on stage." Without that practice, the new skill will feel awkward and appear affected to the audience. One of my clients wrote, "Breathe!" on his notes, but when he did, it was so "scripted" that it looked very unnatural. He needed to practice that off stage until he was ready to perform it on stage.

You need to practice off stage to perform on stage.

Even with a simple skill, like the correct way of breathing, you must get into the habit of doing it the right way off stage because you can't magically switch over to doing it correctly while you speak. Case in point: I was recently doing more research on breathing and came across an author who said not to take a deep breath before speaking. That contradicts everything I've learned and teach, so I dug deeper. What he was describing applied to deep breaths from the chest. *That* will cause your shoulders to tense and your voice to tighten. But the deep "belly breaths" that I teach allow your body to relax and ease your anxieties. If you don't practice deep belly breathing off stage, you'll do shallow chest breathing on stage.

This also demonstrates another key truth. Make sure you're learning the new skills correctly. In high school, I had a friend on the basketball team who was really, really good. A lot of us thought we'd see him playing in college someday. But there was a problem. He'd taught himself some skills incorrectly, and they capped his ability to grow. It was something about the way he threw the ball. It worked fine at the high school level but couldn't carry him much further than that. However, his style was so ingrained—and his identity was so dependent on his success—that he was unwilling to humble himself enough to learn proper technique. His career in basketball ended after the twelfth grade. Let's be humble and take the time to learn new skills, the right way. Use YouTube, learn from more experienced speakers, hire a coach.

LIFETIME LEARNER

Over the rest of this section, I'll give you some skills that will really help you speak with confidence, but there are obviously many, many more. Speaking is multifaceted, and each different type requires different skills, new tools added to your belt. The American philosopher Abraham Kaplan wrote, "Give a small boy a hammer, and he will find that everything he encounters needs pounding."[2] If all you know how to do is give sales presentations, your motivational speeches will sound like a sales pitch. So, I want you to become a student of communication. There will always be more skills to learn—the only limit to how far you go is your interest and need.

Here are my five suggestions for how to add more tools to your belt:

1. Read books and articles about communication.

2. Study other great communicators (such as comedians, politicians, and preachers).

3. Join Toastmasters (an international speaking club).

4. Sign up for my Public Speaking School (use the discount code "SWC" at https://enroll.stepstoadvance.com for an exclusive discount on the Bundle which guides students through all three sources).

5. Volunteer to speak at events.

As I've said, I can't teach you everything. I chose the four skills in the following chapters because they have proven themselves to be immediately helpful to my clients and aren't included in any of my other books.

CHAPTER **15**

The Power of Pauses

NFL superstar Deion Sanders, known for his bling and flashy suits, likes to say, "Look good, feel good. Feel good, play good. Play good, they pay good." On the face of it, wearing a custom-made suit off the field shouldn't make a player catch a football better when he's on it. What Sanders really was talking about was confidence. Anyone making it into the NFL has the ability, but a loss of confidence could neutralize it. Of all the factors (look, feel, play, and pay), looking good is the easiest to control. Addressing that can create an upward spiral of confidence. When you look good, it affects how you feel and . . . you know the rest.

The remaining chapters in Part III will address the way you sound—pauses, filler words, volume, pitch, clarity, and more. Don't dismiss these as inconsequential window dressing compared to the content of the message. Not only are they vital for effectively transmitting your message and holding attention, but (and just as important) they'll help you feel more confident. *Sound* good, feel good. Feel good, play good. Play good, they pay good.

Sound good, feel good. Feel good, play good.
Play good, they pay good.

PAUSES ARE MAGICAL

I was recently holding a communication workshop for an executive team in California, and about halfway through, one of the founders asked, "So, Mike, of all the things you teach, what's the number one thing you tell executives?"

I said, "That's easy. It's . . ." and I paused, waiting as each pair of eyes shifted away from their notes and up at me. "It's pauses."

The founder looked at me for a second then smiled. "Okay, I see what you did."

Pauses are magical. The longer I speak professionally, the better I understand just how powerful and versatile they are. They are one of the most undervalued skills any speaker can develop. Pauses

- . . . create time to think.

- . . . cause people to mentally lean in.

- . . . allow space for people to respond.

- . . . decimate filler words (um, ah, er, and the like).

- . . . make you sound more confident.

- . . . demonstrate mastery and control.

There are three types of pauses that we'll cover in this chapter: (1) the thinking pause, (2) the question pause, and (3) the interest pause.

1. The Thinking Pause

In Chapter 6, I talked about our mental and verbal tracks—your brain is always running in the background and trying to figure out the exact thing to say, how to structure it, and which word to use (the average adult has a vocabulary of 20,000–35,000 to work with). Your brain is fast but not instantaneous. Pauses are essential for accessing its repertoire of words and linking together your chain of thoughts.

The problem is that "nature abhors a vacuum." Meaning, in this case, that (if you're like most people) you're intuitively uncomfortable with the silence created by pauses, so you fill it with the aptly named "filler." There are actually four different types of fillers, listed here in order of increasing distraction.

a. Elongated Words

Just what it sounds like, this means drawing out a word to fill the silence as you mentally develop your next thought. So, you might say, ". . . moving to my next pooooooint . . . ." These aren't too distracting, providing they aren't drawn out comically long.

b. Stammer

Stammering happens as a speaker tries to come up with the next thought and bridges the gap between thoughts by re-re-repeating p-parts of what they are saying. This should not be confused with the speech disorder known as stuttering; instead, stammering is a habit developed as a coping mechanism to fill in spaces between thoughts.

c. Extra Words

This is simply adding extra, unnecessary words. Two common examples are "like" and "just". They don't add anything to the point but attempt to fill in empty space. I once heard an old missionary say "Father" about twenty times in a five-minute blessing over dinner. Transition words are also common offenders: "so," "also," "okay," "as I was saying," "that is to say." I listened to one politician who said "however" at the beginning of nearly every sentence.

Extra words aren't really distracting until you hit a critical mass. Once listeners realize a specific word is your go-to, they'll notice every time you say it. I was speaking at a youth conference not long after becoming a pastor and had a teenager come up afterwards to inform me that I'd said "anyways" twenty-four times—all duly hash-marked in her notebook. She'd been listening intently but not for the right thing!

d. Ah's and Um's

Listeners notice these quicker than the other types because they have no inherent meaning. They're so problematic that at Toastmasters, they assign an "Ah Counter" at every meeting to report on all such fillers. More than any of the others, these are seen as demonstrations of insecurity and rob you of authority.

My wife and I are avid watchers of *America's Got Talent*. In this reality show/talent contest, any of the judges (but usually Simon Cowell) can hit the red buzzer during the performance if they don't like it. In my mind, every "um" effectively hits a red buzzer in the listeners' head. Initially, it's so quiet that they don't consciously notice, but it still pulls attention away from your message. The buzzer gets a little louder each time until it passes a threshold. Then the listener actively notices every "um." It continues to get louder and requires increasing effort for your listener to regain focus.

Every "um" effectively hits a red buzzer in the listener's head.

AWARENESS

Think through your most recent speech or presentation. What type of fillers were you most inclined to use? Try recording a presentation and being your own "Ah Counter."

I bring up fillers now, in the middle of our discussion about Thinking Pauses, because intentionally pausing is the best antidote to fillers. I've discovered that most people use fillers because they're afraid that even a moment of silence in their speech will:

- Break their train of thought,

- Disrupt their flow,

- Make them look unintelligent, or

- Cause the audience to lose interest

That's not how it works. As I said earlier, a pause is simply a vacuum, and vacuums long to be filled. Instead of *you* filling it with fillers, allow the *audience* to fill it with curiosity. Said another way, vacuums create space that's filled with their attention. Think of the story I told at the beginning of this point. If I had answered the founder's question immediately, he might have been the only person to hear it, and even he wouldn't have been as interested; my pause increased interest. I'm going to talk about the Interest Pause in just a little bit, but I need to assure you now that Thinking Pauses do not lose attention—listeners subconsciously lean in deeper to hear what you're going to say next.

Pauses create a vacuum that's filled with the audience's attention.

Like many people, you may already be aware of your fillers and want to get rid of them. The problem is that the more you think about not using fillers, the more likely you are to use them. When you were a new driver and were afraid of running into the oncoming cars, you would keep thinking, "Don't cross the yellow line. Don't cross the yellow line," which caused you to veer toward it even more. Don't focus on subtracting fillers, but think about adding Thinking Pauses instead. The best way to replace fillers with Thinking Pauses is slowing down and intentionally inserting pauses when you need to gather your thoughts. A lot of my clients don't like this advice because it feels incredibly unnatural at first, but (if they trust me) they soon find themselves back at full speed, without the fillers.

Don't focus on subtracting fillers but adding Thinking Pauses instead.

Practice

Find an old presentation or speech of yours and give it in front of a mirror, but slow down enough to add Thinking Pauses (instead of fillers) whenever you need to plan your next words. Remember, practice off stage to perform on stage.

---

2. The Question/Response Pause

Not long after the co-founder of that California company asked me for my best communication tip, I had an opportunity to demonstrate another "magical" power of the pause. I asked what was clearly a rhetorical question then waited long enough for the silence to become awkward. They looked at me, but I just took a sip of water. Eventually, someone asked, "Did you want us to respond?"

"Thank you," I said. "You just proved my point. If you pause long enough, somebody will eventually answer."

Pauses don't just allow you to process your own thoughts (Thinking Pause); they also allow the audience to process their own thoughts and respond. Even if you aren't looking for an actual answer to a question, it still allows them to respond internally. One mark of an experienced speaker is knowing when to pause, so the audience can process and internalize what's been said. Remember: A speech isn't like a book. Your audience can't go back and "reread" something that requires extra thought. You have to do that for them.

Pauses allow the audience to process their own thoughts and respond.

I'm not going to spend a lot of time on this because I covered it in my book *Speak & Meet Virtually* (which also has very practical tips for real-life meetings, including how—and whether—to encourage audience participation), but we frequently prevent our listeners from responding by not giving sufficient time to do so.

Here's an important dynamic to understand. The longer you talk, the more your listeners shift into a passive mode. Coming out of that mode takes time. Think about the last time you were in an hour-long meeting and the presenter ended with "Are there any questions?"—followed by five seconds of looking around the room—then saying, "I guess not." It takes five seconds just to mentally register that he's asking for questions, never mind formulating a question and gathering the courage to speak up. That presenter effectively made it clear that he didn't *want* to answer any questions.

If you want people to ask you questions or respond to questions that you posed to them, simply wait until they do. Let *them* fill the vacuum of silence. I also like to call this the Awkward Pause. One company I worked with loved the term so much it became part of their vernacular. The speaker will literally say, "Now, I'm going to awkwardly pause." It gets a laugh—and results.

If you want people to respond, wait until they do.

This technique also demonstrates great confidence (even if you're not feeling it). One trick is having some sort of business to do while you're waiting, such as taking a sip of water or flipping through notes.

AWARENESS AND PRACTICE

Think back on a recent presentation that was supposed to involve audience participation. On a scale of 1 to 10, how did you feel about their level of participation?

In your next presentation, practice the art of the Awkward Pause. Bonus tip: Tell the audience your expectations in advance. Encourage them to write down their questions as you talk or to put them in the chat box (if it's a virtual meeting).

---

3. The Interest Pause

When it comes to writing, one of the things an editor looks for is variety in the length and structure of sentences. Too many long, complicated sentences become laborious to read. Too many short, simple sentences become boring. The same is true in speaking, but instead of punctuation, you use things like tonal variations and silence. We're going to talk about cadence and speaking pace in a couple of chapters, but I want to address the role of pauses now.

I talked earlier about *America's Got Talent* and the red buzzer, and how it kills interest. Now, think about the host, Terry Crews, getting ready to announce the final results. He doesn't rush through but skillfully increases anticipation through pauses. The producers pull it out even longer with carefully timed commercial breaks. You know how it goes: You're waiting on the edge of your seat, Terry's lips finally start to move, and then the theme music plays over his voice, and you throw something at the TV. You knew it was coming, but it still gets you.

Skillful speakers know how to use pauses to increase antici-pation. This could almost be called a dramatic pause because you are being dramatic. Used correctly, it can add interests to almost anything—even financial reports:

"Last quarter was great . . ." [pause, pause some more. Eyes begin to focus on you] ". . . and this quarter was even better."

Obviously, you want to use the Interest Pause strategically. Long pauses followed by something not worth waiting for will get you parodied at the company Christmas party. Consider using it for:

- Key transitions,
- Significant points,
- Before or after statements that resonate emotionally, or
- Before your conclusion.

Skillful speakers know how to use pauses to increase anticipation.

There's a next-level version of this, inspired by my favorite story about the Dalai Lama. He was running late for a speaking engagement but wanted to find a way to honor the audience and connect with them. He walked in without saying a word and, one by one, silently greeted each person with eye contact and a smile. He did more than connect—he created intense anticipation for his speech. I tried a similar strategy when I spoke to a room of professionals and found that, because of the anticipation I built, I was able to shorten my planned introduction and get into the meat of what I was saying. But, again, this is a "next-level" skill because it requires great confidence. If *you* feel awkward, the audience will as well. And use it very sparingly. If even one person in a group has seen you do it twice, it may feel very insincere.

AWARENESS AND PRACTICE

First, practice by reading aloud from a book and finding places to use all three types of pauses (Thinking, Response, and Interest). Experiment by moving pauses to different places and get a feel for how meaning changes.

Second, use what you just learned to find strategic places to pause in your next presentation and literally write "PAUSE" in your notes.

Finally, build awareness by recording that presentation and observing what worked and what didn't. Don't be embarrassed by what didn't work—just learn from it.

Do you like your voice? Do you find that people frequently ask you to repeat yourself? As a speaker, your voice is your single most important instrument, so clarity is a crucial skill to master. That's what we'll work on next.

CHAPTER 16

Voice and Clarity

A violin that's missing half its strings, a clarinet with a broken reed, and a piano that hasn't been tuned since the Clinton administration—those instruments that are not going to make good music regardless of how talented the musician is. As a speaker, your voice is your instrument, and it needs to be in good working order. Furthermore, if you're not confident in your instrument, you won't be confident in your speaking.

Your voice is your instrument.

In this chapter, I'll teach you vital skills for fine-tuning your voice, starting with how it sounds and moving to things like articulation and accents.

CAN I CHANGE MY VOICE?

My clients often ask me if they can change their voice. It usually comes on the heels of evaluating a recording of their speech. It's an experience we're all familiar with. Our voice just sounds wrong when we hear what everyone else hears. Before answering their question, I explain why it sounds so different. When we talk, we simultaneously hear our voice two different ways: the vibrations that travel through our jawbone and into our ear canal plus the sound coming through the air, but at an odd angle (because our mouth is pointed away from our ears). So, when you hear your own voice, you're literally hearing more than others do. And when others speak, they're hearing more of their voice than you do. With practice, singers learn how to mentally adjust for that difference, and you can do the same over time. Don't try to make adjustments to your voice until you're able to evaluate it through the ears of others.

That said, there are three things you can do about the sound of your voice:

1. **Micro-Change**
   This is simply the learned habit of speaking in a slightly higher or lower pitch than your natural voice. The emphasis is on "slightly." You cannot turn yourself into a James Earl Jones; attempting to do so will sound unnatural and can actually damage your voice. But you can shift your "normal" pitch the same way you'd change your posture—intentionally speak in a way that doesn't feel quite natural until it becomes your new normal. This is what I did in my twenties because I felt my voice wasn't authoritative enough. I continually practiced speaking a little bit lower, reading books out loud, giving speeches, and monitoring my conversations until it became my new habit. Even still, my voice will occasionally go back to its original pitch when I get excited.

2. **Modulate**
   We're going to talk more about pitch in the next chapter, but modulation means temporarily changing your tone to match the setting, like speaking in a higher pitch to a baby or lowering it with someone who is grieving. Unlike the practiced habit of micro-change, modulation is an intentional fluctuation that is part of your expressiveness.

3. **Power Up**

    I spend a lot of time discussing breathing in other books, so I don't want to repeat myself too much, but you need to understand that your lungs are your voice's power supply. If you're slouched over in a chair, your voice will likely sound weak and powerless. If you stand up and fill your lungs from the bottom (below the diaphragm), your voice will have more power available. So, if you're unhappy with your voice's strength, start by giving it plenty of air. I invested in a special desk that raises and lowers with the push of a button, so that I can easily stand to record a teaching video or give a Zoom presentation. This effectively helps me power up my voice. Powering up is also the key to projecting your voice, that is, increasing your voice's volume without screaming.

Your lungs are your voice's power supply.

WHAT DID YOU SAY?

As a kid, my doctor was a very capable and friendly man, but he hadn't learned English until later in life, and I didn't always understand him. I was pretty sure I heard him "well enough" and was too embarrassed to ask, "I'm sorry, what was that?" I'm sure you've had a similar experience.

    Your voice is kind of like the smell of your breath. It's such a personal thing that most people won't tell you if it's bad. Likewise, they usually won't tell you if they can't understand you—at least once you're out of junior high (those little jerks have no problem laughing at funny accents or speech impediments). Just because no one has said anything, doesn't mean you don't need to pay attention. Like with bad breath, you must learn how to check yourself and get good at reading nonverbal clues, like a quizzical expression (or extra "social distancing," in the case of bad breath).

AWARENESS

Listen to past presentations, paying attention to clarity. Could you understand every word? If you feel you're lacking in clarity, involve some others, but don't ask questions like, "Can you understand me?" Instead, try safer-to-answer ones like, "What percentage of the time are you unsure of what I said?", then double their answer.

Don't be too quick to give yourself a pass on this skill. Most of my clients need to give at least some attention to their clarity. Understand that "good enough" isn't good enough. It's not enough if they can figure out what you're saying; they need to understand you effortlessly. Any bandwidth your listeners spend deciphering your words is bandwidth they don't have for your message. This skill has become even more crucial for virtual meetings because lack of physical presence, the inherent laziness of the medium, and the mediocrity of many microphones make you even harder to understand.

Any bandwidth your listeners spend deciphering your words is bandwidth they don't have for your message.

Before I go any further, let's clarify my terms. By clarity, I mean people being able to clearly understand you; what you meant is what the listener hears (assuming they don't have a hearing problem). This could be called elocution, but that tends to bring up images of Dr. Henry Higgins in *My Fair Lady*. Clarity includes:

- Projection: speaking with enough power to be heard.
- Enunciation: speaking words and sentences fully, clearly, and plainly.
- Articulation: the formation of clear and distinct sounds.
- Pronunciation: saying words the correct way.

CLARITY KILLERS

A speech impediment, having to learn a new language when my family moved to Mexico, and braces in an age before Invisalign— these things conspired to kill my clarity. My mom was always my biggest coach. She pushed me further than I was willing to push myself, and without her support, I wonder whether I'd ever have become a public speaker. After high school, I moved back to Washington to attend university and was excited to invite her to a big Christmas play I was in. It was the biggest thing I'd done— five performances to a packed auditorium of 1,000 people each show.

Before the show, my mom came up to wish me luck, and I could sense her mixture of pride and concern. The last thing she said to me was, "Mike, just make sure to open your mouth, okay?"

"Okay, Mom," I said as I suppressed a grin. Joining a nationally ranked collegiate debate team had taught me a thing or two since she'd last heard me speak publicly. When she came up to me after the performance, she was beaming but also a little confused. "You didn't mumble! I could understand every word. What happened?"

What happened was that I'd finally understood her lessons and learned several more from our nationally respected debate coach. With their help, and through continued study, I've learned how to combat the three "clarity killers" with specific "clarity fixers."

1. The Half-Opened Mouth

I've already mentioned my braces but didn't tell you why I had them or how bad they were. You know that vintage late '80s yearbook picture of a kid with buckteeth teeth that would make a horse jealous and braces that looked like an instrument of torture? That was me, or easily could have been. As a result, I tried to keep them hidden behind a barely open mouth whenever I felt put on the spot. In extreme situations, I was even known to cover my mouth when I talked.

Even after my dentist extracted four "extra" teeth, and my braces came and went, I retained the habit of barely opening my mouth to talk. That's why my mom always reminded me: "Stop mumbling, and open your mouth!" I like to illustrate the importance of following that advice in my coaching by holding a book in front of my mouth while I speak. It's almost like a game in my mind to see how long until my clients ask me to put it down. After they do, I tell them that almost everyone effectively covers their mouth when they talk. But instead of a book, it's covered by their lips and teeth. Here's a key principle: Your lips are the valves that regulate the power of your lungs. If they aren't opened all the way, your audience isn't getting everything you have to give.

Your lips are the valves that regulate the power of your lungs.

During the opening credits of Will Ferrell's movie *Anchorman*, Ron Burgundy is seen exercising his lips by saying, "How now, brown cow." While played up for comedy, exercises like that are commonly used by actors and professional speakers. There are over a dozen muscle groups in your face that play some role in your mouth's movement. Most of the time, they are relaxed and "like" staying that way. They need to be stretched for you to gain their full use.

AWARENESS AND PRACTICE

First, speak some simple line out loud, like "Hi, my name is _____. It's very nice to meet you." Now, say "How now, brown cow," a couple of times, over-pronouncing it and opening your lips as wide as possible. Notice how much stretching you feel. Then repeat the first phrase. Did you notice how much more easily your mouth formed the words?

Get into the habit of going through some mouth stretches throughout the day, especially just before talking on the phone or giving a presentation. I'll give you another one for exercising your tongue shortly.

So, the clarity killer is a half-opened mouth, and the clarity fixer comes straight from my mom—don't forget to open your mouth! This allows you to both project your voice with more power (by opening the valve) and to improve your enunciation. By stretching all those mouth muscles, you prepare them to move better for each word.

While this clarity fixer is aimed at your mouth and enunciation, it's foundational to addressing the next clarity killer, which has to do with your tongue. Imagine trying to do yoga in a coat closet; you just won't be able to stretch nearly as far as you need to. The same is true of your tongue. To work its best, you need to let it stretch beyond the confines of a half-opened mouth.

2. Speech Impediment

As a kid, my tongue just couldn't do its part to create the "j" sound; it always came out as "sh" or "ch." My parents had me work with a speech therapist, and among other things she gave me exercises for strengthening my tongue and lips. My mom then dedicated herself to coaching me and encouraging me when I got discouraged. As a result, it hasn't been an issue since.

Genuine speech impediments are a very real thing with various causes, so I'm not saying that anyone with one just needs to work harder. Instead, I'm using "speech impediment" in a more informal sense here. Many, if not most, people struggle to articulate their words because their tongues are being a little lazy. I mentioned earlier that my editor is an experienced speaker. He realized early on that articulation was a real problem for him, so he decided to work with a speech therapist. Initially, she was confused why someone without an actual speech impediment wanted to work with her (and the hospital's billing department had no idea what to do with him). But once she understood his objectives, she enthusiastically worked with him to improve his clarity. His biggest issue? A lazy tongue that didn't "want" to pronounce every syllable. He was surprised to discover that "probably" had three syllables—prob-ab-bly instead of prob-ly.

To help him exercise all the muscles in his tongue and mouth, she had him practice saying this classic speech therapy test because it utilizes almost every sound in English:

> You wished to know all about my grandfather. Well, he is nearly ninety-three years old. He dresses himself each day in an ancient black frock coat, usually minus several buttons; yet he still thinks as swiftly as ever. A long, flowing beard clings to his chin, giving those who observe him a pronounced feeling of the utmost respect. When he speaks, his voice is just a bit cracked and quivers a trifle. Twice each day he plays skillfully and with

zest upon our small organ. Except in the winter when the ooze or snow or ice prevents, he slowly takes a short walk in the open air each day. We have often urged him to walk more and smoke less, but he always answers, "Banana Oil!" Grandfather likes to be modern in his language.

He was initially frustrated because his muscles refused to make all the required sounds, and his tongue would literally be fatigued after reading through it a couple times. He began practicing every day in the car. Slowly, his muscles strengthened, and he could pronounce every syllable with precision. Even still, he continues to use it as a warm-up whenever he prepares to speak.

AWARENESS AND PRACTICE

Try reading the "Grandfather" paragraph, being careful to pronounce each syllable. How did you do? If it was easy, then you may have already developed this skill sufficiently. If not, read through it multiple times a day, focusing on accuracy instead of speed.

Another great articulation exercise is saying, "The tip of the tongue, the roof of the mouth, the lips and the teeth." I learned this one in college drama class. We'd use it as part of our warm-up, saying it really fast, then slowly, then in a high pitch, followed by a low pitch. Cycling through that a couple times forced us to focus on many key sounds and increased our tongues' dexterity.

Speech impediments are the clarity killer, and exercising your mouth and tongue is the clarity fixer. Just talking a lot does not count as exercise any more than splashing around in a pool will help you swim the 100 meters at the Olympics. Improving your articulation requires concerted and specific training. There are forty-four different sounds (called phonemes) in the English language, and each one of them has a specific way it needs to be pronounced—put your tongue here, move your lips thus, and so on. As I said, the grandfather paragraph is used by therapists to assess their client's specific challenges. You can likewise use it to isolate the phonemes that you need to focus on. (To be clear, I'm not a speech therapist, and so I can't make any professional recommendations, but there are many great tools and exercises available online.)

Remember—practice off stage what you want to do on stage. Make this skill a priority, and your listeners (along with family and coworkers) will thank you.

3. Accents and ESL

I've had several clients who want me to help them get rid of their accent. I tell them, "Don't get rid of it because it's part of who you are! It makes you an individual." Instead, I have them focus on increasing clarity without changing their identity. This is true whether you have a southern drawl or a thick Scottish accent or learned English as a second language

Focus on increasing clarity without changing identity.

The challenge in every situation is to identify which sounds, pronunciations, and words make it harder to be understood by your audience. Those last two items apply more to accents than ESL. Americans and Brits, for instance, are well-known for using words differently. Having worked with missionaries around the world, I have watched a lot of humorous misunderstandings, like when a Brit asks a Yankee (as we're called) if they have a rubber (eraser). Even in America, regional pronunciations can vary so much that we sometimes struggle to understand each other. Again, don't try to eliminate all distinctive words or sounds, just the distractions.

Specific sounds, on the other hand, can create a significant challenge to non-native speakers. As we've been saying, your tongue is a muscular organ, and it may struggle to make a sound it's never had to. When I first moved to Mexico, I struggled with rolling my R sounds, so my mom found a language coach to focus on developing and strengthening my Spanish skills. This wasn't simply an accent issue; it was a clarity issue because it affects the meaning of certain words. "*Pero*," for instance, means "but," while "*perro*" (rolled R) means dog. Over the course of several months, my coach had me practice rolling my R sounds over and over again until I could say *perro* and *pero* correctly without thinking about it.

Having an accent and speaking English as a second language are the potential clarity killers, and the clarity fixer is targeted attention on the sounds, pronunciations, and words that cause miscommunication. Remember, the goal isn't losing your accent but gaining clarity. Celebrate your heritage. Cherish your first language. It is part of who you are. And work to make it easier for your listeners to understand you.

AWARENESS AND PRACTICE

Ask someone to listen to a presentation of yours and identify any places where they struggled to understand you. With that information, make note of the words and sounds you need to work on. Look online for resources that target your specific needs. If, for instance, your first language is Hindi, look for diction videos on YouTube by other ESL Indians. Practice the unfamiliar sounds until they feel familiar.

AN EXTRA ARTICULATION AND ENUNCIATION EXERCISE

I said earlier that my mom was worried she wouldn't be able to understand me when she came to my Christmas performance. My debate coach had the same concerns when I first joined the team but knew how to help. "Hey, Mike," he said. "I've got an exercise I want you to do." He treated it like no big deal—soccer players are expected to run several miles a day, and the debate club members were expected to exercise their mouths. His exercise was what allowed me to shock my mom that evening. It's a fantastic tool, and I now use it with many of my clients.

He told me to put a pencil in my mouth, so that it restricted my tongue, and practice talking. I went back to the dorms, stood in front of a mirror, chomped down, and began reading out of a book. I felt really silly—especially because of the slobber running out of the edges of my lips—and would take the pencil out whenever someone walked by. I could feel my tongue, jaw, and mouth getting a real workout and had to stop after a couple minutes, but I kept practicing daily for the next several months and weekly for the next couple of years. I'll still do it occasionally when I feel like I've regressed a little.

There are three different places where you can put the pencil, each exercising a different set of muscles. Visit content. mikeacker.com for a video demonstration. It's crucial to understand that this isn't a one-time exercise. I recommend doing it once a day for three months. I had one client buy 100 #2 pencils (their softness makes them a good choice) and use one a day, discarding it afterward. After 100 days of this exercise, the change was evident to everyone he worked with just as my change had been to my mom.

I don't know about you, but I'd much rather listen to speakers who struggle with clarity but use great variety in how they speak—high crescendos and dramatic lows, speeding up with excitement and slowing down for emphasis—than someone with perfect articulation but a monotone voice. Ideally, speakers have both. Learning to speak with vocal variety is a vital skill both for engaging interest and illuminating your message. We'll cover that in the next chapter.

CHAPTER 17

Vocal Variety

Thanks to my social media feed, I recently came across the following humorous reviews for instructors on "Rate My Professor":

> "Bring a pillow to the class, so when you lose consciousness, your head won't slam on your desk, and bring a pillow for your pillow because your pillow will fall asleep, too."
>
> "Boring but I learned there are 137 tiles on the ceiling."
>
> "I don't wear my seat belt driving to school because I want to die before I make it to this class."

Can you relate to any of these? We've all had teachers like those, ones who drone on and on. We describe them as dull, dry, or uninteresting, but the best description is *monotone*. Maybe they're saying different words, but they all sound (tone) the same (mono). It doesn't matter if that sound is high or low, fast or slow, loud or quiet, it will sound monotonous if there isn't any variety.

Here's why vocal variety is crucial. In every waking moment, your brain is bombarded by a massive amount of stimulation and information, so it has to sort between the irrelevant (such as the sound of the traffic) and the vital (a car swerving in your direction). It does this by filtering out things that stay the same and focusing on things that change. We are wired to ignore the monotonous. This is why you will so quickly adapt to an obnoxious smell in your house—or a droning speech. Your brain is literally trying to save your life by pushing boring or repetitive stimulus into the background.

We are wired to ignore the monotonous.

In my experience, monotonous speaking is usually caused by (1) no longer caring about your topic and/or what your audience thinks of you, (2) a total lack of confidence, or (3) not having the necessary skills to avoid it. I know you're not in the first category because you're reading this book. I trust that the work we've already done has largely dealt with the second. So, the purpose of this chapter is to address number three.

In the previous chapter, I talked about clarity—things like enunciation and articulation. All that falls under the umbrella of diction, which is the entirety of your manner or style of speaking. Another component of diction is vocal variety, which includes elements such as:

- Intonation: the rise and fall of your voice's pitch. It can be measured by hertz. You have a natural range which can be affected by things, such as mood or stress.

- Inflection: a near synonym for intonation, but more narrowly focused on pitch changes within a word or short phrase, such as the increased pitch as the end of a sentence to signal a question.

- Volume: the loudness or amplitude of your voice. This is measured by decibels.

- Velocity: the speed at which you speak, measured by words per minute.

- Pauses: intentional breaks within your talking for the purpose of variation and emphasis, etc. (see Chapter 15).

- Emphasis: stress made on a word or phrase, usually through an increase of inflection and velocity.

Taken together, all the components of diction—how you say something—say something about you. They become part of the way you demonstrate your identity. Furthermore, there is no one right diction. Just as there are many different kinds of boats that serve various purposes, there are many different kinds of speakers and ways of speaking. My goal here is not to turn out a bunch of cookie cutter speed boats but help you be the best boat—I mean, speaker—you can be.

How you say something says something about you.

At the same time, your diction isn't just an extension of your identity; it is also part of your message. It can draw in your audience or deter them. This is why you can't just say, "This is how I talk." You have to do the work of improving your vocal variety or else risk ending up like one of those boring teachers you dreaded.

THE VOCAL VARIETY GRID

I've developed the following "vocal variety grid" to help my clients add depth to their diction without changing who they are.

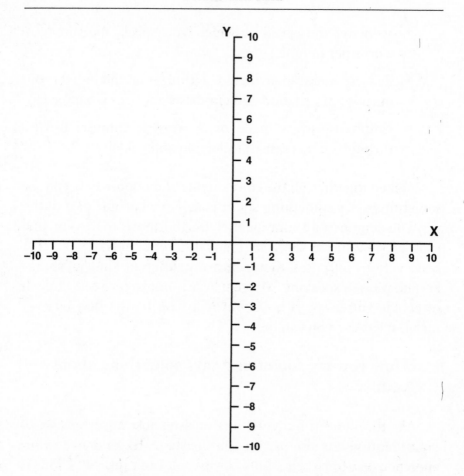

On the above grid, the X axis is your pace, which is your velocity and usage of pauses. The Y axis is your energy, which is the combination of your volume and relative intonation (pitch). The term "relative" is important because intonation has to be measured against your own range, not the range of all humans. Even when I am speaking at the upper end of my intonation, it is still lower in hertz than many women speaking at the bottom of theirs.

AWARENESS

First, examine your pace. Are you a fast or slow talker? Do your words tend to run together, or are you more like the sloths on *Zootopia*? Place yourself on the X axis, with –10 being the slowest pace, 0 average, and 10 fastest.

Second, think about your energy. Do you tend to talk in the top, middle, or bottom of your range? Are you naturally the loudest or quietest person in the room? Place yourself on the Y axis, with –10 being the lowest energy, 0 average, and 10 highest.

Now, ask some others to answer those questions about you, but without showing them your answers. Adjust your answer accordingly, and once you're confident about the results, mark the place where your X and Y intersect. This is your natural starting point.

I'm about a 4 on energy and a 3 on pace, so my natural starting point would look like this:

Once you know your natural starting place, we can look at the four quadrants this grid creates:

- Quadrant 1: High energy and slow pace
- Quadrant 2: High energy and fast pace
- Quadrant 3: Low energy and fast pace
- Quadrant 4: Low energy and slow pace

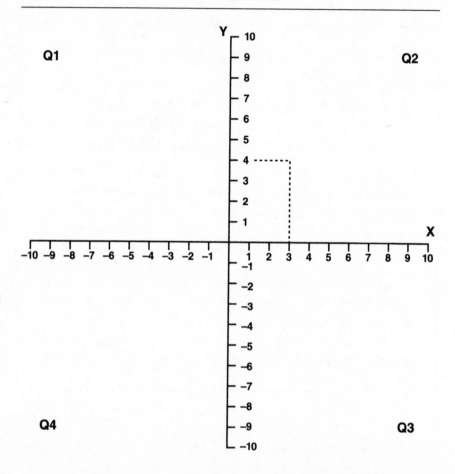

Going back to what we said about identity, it's vital to understand that no quadrant is inherently better than another, and any of them can be monotonous. Whichever one you fall into is perfect for you—as a starting point. In fact, I want you to mentally shift the entire grid, so that the 0,0 point (where the X and Y axes meet) now sits at *your* starting point. The goal of this grid is to help you move through the different quadrants, relative to your own starting point.

Each quadrant is important and has a particular purpose:

1. **Quadrant 1: High energy and slow pace**
   Together, high and slow convey a commanding presence. The slower speed allows you to convey more

details while the higher energy conveys importance. Think of a high school principal giving an important announcement that is detail-laden. This quadrant is also good for a unifying message or issuing a critique or correction.

2. **Quadrant 2: High energy and fast pace**
   This is the party quadrant. It engages people and is full of excitement. Its high energy creates excitement but makes it unsuitable for conveying fine details. This is how you would announce the breaking of sales records and other good news.

3. **Quadrant 3: Low energy and fast pace**
   This communicates urgency under control. It's like, "Houston, we have a problem." If that iconic statement had been conveyed high and fast, it would've invited panic. Low and fast models calm in face of an emergency. It orders people to lean in and get to work.

4. **Quadrant 4: Low energy and slow pace**
   This is the calming quadrant. It's what you would hear from the staff at a high-end restaurant or hotel. Counselors use this, and teach it to their clients. Likewise, this is what a police officer will use to de-escalate a situation or talk someone out of jumping off a bridge. It's also effective for correcting people in a nonthreatening way.

MOVING AROUND THE GRID

As I said, each of these quadrants is important and has a specific purpose. Imagine using the extremities of the quadrants in the wrong situation—like an officer using high and fast with a potential jumper. Not quite as bad is moving through the quadrants aimlessly in an ineffective attempt to "increase vocal variety." The quadrant must match the message. A mismatched message will confuse and distract your audience while lowering your authority.

The quadrant must match the message.

You start from your personal baseline (0,0) and move from there into the various quadrants but at an appropriate intensity. By that, I mean some content may call for a slight increase in energy and pace (for instance), but others should have you practically shouting for joy. Here are some examples of possible content and quadrant matches:

- A speech's introduction: High and fast.
- Important details: High and slow.
- Quick overview of bullet points: Low and fast.
- Allowing the audience to absorb a point: Low and slow.
- Announcing new product or solution: High and slow.
- Conclusion to a motivational speech: High and slow.

PRACTICE

I want you to first practice the mechanics of the quadrants without worrying about meaning. Find a book, and practice reading one short paragraph in each quadrant. Again, don't think about whether or not the material matches meaning—I want you to get comfortable speaking in each of the four ways.

When I do this with my clients, I ask them to really stretch themselves, but they usually think they're stretching much further than they are. What they think is a 10 is closer to a 3. You have to push yourself to what feels comically high/low/fast/slow in order to make a perceivable change.

After you've practiced the mechanics, add in connecting the quadrant with meaning. Read through a recent or upcoming speech or presentation. Look for places that naturally fit in the different quadrants and mark them with H/S, H/F, L/F, or L/S, or maybe highlight them in different colors. Then practice the speech out loud. Experiment with using various quadrants in various places. Notice how the meaning changes.

THE Z FACTOR

Perhaps you noticed that the Vocal Variety Grid covers things like volume and velocity but not emphasis and inflection. These are what I call "the Z Factor." This punches off the grid into another dimension by adding a burst of energy to a phrase, word, or syllable. Those of you who are old enough may remember Jolt soda back in the mid-'80s with its slogan, "All of the sugar and twice the caffeine." That's how you can think of the Z Factor, a little extra jolt to increase energy. Again, this adds another dimension to your speaking while drawing attention to key ideas. But, just like an energy drink, you want to go easy on them. Too much will leave your listener's head buzzing.

The Z Factor adds another dimension to your speaking while drawing attention to key ideas.

Emphasis (the Z Factor) can be achieved by:

- Stretching out the vowel of the word.
- Putting the inflection on the first syllable.

- Speaking slower for the word or phrase.
- Pausing after the word or phrase.

AWARENESS AND PRACTICE

Build awareness by reading the following sentence multiple times, successively emphasizing each word. Notice how significantly the meaning changes (a key follows if you struggle to find the new meanings):

"John isn't driving to Seattle today."

Key:

- John: Someone else is driving to Seattle.
- Isn't: His plans have changed, and he isn't driving at all.
- Driving: He's getting to Seattle another way.
- To: Seattle isn't the destination. Maybe he's driving from or through it.
- Seattle: He's driving somewhere other than Seattle.
- Today: He's driving on a different day.

Now, practice this by finding a key sentence in an upcoming speech and reading it out loud, emphasizing a different word each time. How did the meaning change? Which word do you want to give the Z Factor?

Another exercise I use with my TEDx clients is to have them grab a book, highlight one word per sentence, and read it out loud, emphasizing the highlighted word.

AVOID UPTALK

Also in the movie *Anchorman*, the teleprompter accidentally added a question mark to the phrase, "I'm Ron Burgundy?" and Ron—who always says, on air, exactly what's on the teleprompter—adds the "down then up" inflection used to denote questions. It's a humorous moment in the movie, but it's less funny when people do it in real life. This is commonly called uptalk, defined as "a style of speech in which every sentence ends with a rising tone, as if the speaker is always asking a question."

Everyone uses uptalk occasionally, especially when they lack confidence in their statement, but some people (about 20% of my clients) do it habitually. In my experience, it's more common among women than men but by no means exclusively so.

Uptalk is a negative type of vocal variety you need to actively avoid—especially when giving a speech. Unless you mean to ask a question, you should make a statement. When you intone a sentence to sound like a question, it communicates uncertainty and diminishes authority. Here is how I like to illustrate it to my clients: I tell them to ask me my favorite movie. They usually laugh uncertainly then ask, "Mike, what's your favorite movie?"

I respond, *"The Usual Suspects,"* only I drop my inflection just a touch on "sus" and bring it up on "pects." I call this the valley inflection, down and then up. The result is that it sounds like I'm not sure if that's a good answer. It's almost like I'm seeking permission to like the most amazing movie ever.

Then I have them ask me again. This time I respond, *"The Usual Suspects,"* bringing my tone up a touch on "sus" and landing "pects" on a solid downward inflection. Without changing my words, I've effectively added, "And I don't care what you think."

When you make a statement sound like a
question, it communicates uncertainty and
diminishes authority.

AWARENESS AND PRACTICE

Because this is such an ingrained habit for many, it's hard
for them to even be aware of it. Start listening to other
people, and see if you can detect uptalk, ask people who
know you well if you do it, and listen to your own presentations. Pay particular attention to when you're most
prone to uptalk. When you're expressing your opinion?
When you're unsure of your answer? When talking to a
supervisor?

In your own head, picture a red buzzer, like on
America's Got Talent, and press it every time you hear anyone (yourself included) do it. Again, you're just trying to
build awareness at this point. For some of my clients, this
is sufficient—once you listen for it, it sounds kind of
funny. But for others, their uptalk is rooted in insecurity.
In this case, the following practices are often sufficient,
but sometimes professional counseling is needed to dig
out root causes.

Work on slashing your uptalk in daily conversations.
Maybe enlist the help of your partner or a close friend
and establish a secret signal for when you do it. Practice
off stage what you want to occur on stage. Think through
the situations where you're most likely to use uptalk and
practice those, out loud and in front of a mirror, as statements. Visualize coming down a mountain and landing
solidly on your feet at the end of a sentence.

True confidence, I've been saying, is built not just on the foundation of who you are (identity) and the content of what you say (message), but also the skills you use—a deficiency here can negate any gains you make in the first two areas. This is especially true of the next skill I'm going to teach you: nonverbal communication.

CHAPTER 18

Nonverbals

Various studies have shown that the majority of our communication occurs nonverbally.[1] In her 2012 TED Talk, Dr. Amy Cuddy cited two studies that made that statement more concrete to me. First, Nalini Ambady (Tufts University), showed people 30-second *soundless* clips of actual physician-patient interactions and had them rate the physician's niceness. Those ratings were able to accurately predict whether or not that physician would be sued. Second, Alex Todorov (Princeton University) has found that participants' judgments of a political candidate's face, after watching for *one second*, predicted the results of 70% of U.S. Senate and gubernatorial races.

How you say something is part of the message itself, for example, rolling your eyes while saying "Nice job" fundamentally shifts the meaning. What you do with your body (especially your face) has the power to improve or destroy the effectiveness of your speech or presentation, making nonverbal communication skills nonnegotiable. You can't focus solely on *saying* something but must also work on *showing* something. A lot has been written on this topic, and this chapter isn't a comprehensive treatment. Instead, I've focused on the skills my clients have found most helpful.

Nonverbal communication skills are nonnegotiable.

This skill is especially crucial because, as I've said many times, the insecurity of communication comes from its uncertainty. Specifically, many of my clients struggle with the uncertainty of what to do with their hands, where to look, and so forth. Your non-verbals convey a lot about your confidence—or lack thereof—to your audience. As you improve this skill, your confidence will grow.

THREE PRINCIPLES OF NONVERBAL COMMUNICATION

Technically, nonverbal communication includes diction, but we covered that in the previous chapter, so I'm using it here to refer to communication that doesn't come from the mouth. In this chapter, we're going to work on areas of (1) facial expressions, (2) hand gestures, and (3) physical movement. But, first, there are three key principles for the confident use of nonverbals.

1. Your Movement Must Match Your Words

In the same way that a mismatch between the content and the vocal variety quadrant will confuse the listener and undermine your authority, so must your nonverbals match your message. I was working with one client who appeared really serious all the time, so I worked with her to smile more—until she smiled all the way through a speech about a difficult life situation. Served me right, I guess. Obviously, I needed to clarify. Smile more, yes, but not if it contradicts your content.

There is also a confidence-building effect of this principle: When your words and your movements are in alignment, they build on each other and create greater power and excitement within you. It just feels right.

One caveat/pro tip here: When your content, diction, and nonverbals are all in alignment, they can exude a massive amount of power, especially with a more serious or negative message. Be careful not to overdo it. Imagine, for instance, that you have to reprimand your team. It's a serious matter and needs to change, but they don't need to be hit with both barrels. Don't water down the content; that will make you look insecure and uncertain. Boldly and confidently communicate what you need to communicate. Don't modify your diction significantly either. That will confuse your teams, leaving them unsure if you're serious. Instead, lighten your nonverbals by avoiding a severe expression and utilizing open gestures (we'll get there shortly). This approach will allow you to convey your message with clarity but without blowing your team away.

If, however, you *are* furious and the situation requires both barrels (such as their not having responded to the previous approach), then hit them with that full-powered alignment of content, diction, and nonverbals.

2. You Control Your Body, Not the Other Way Around

Whether it's rocking on your feet like an upside-down pendulum or unconsciously fidgeting with a pen, your habits and nervous energy are looking for ways to get out, distracting the audience and embarrassing you. You have to learn how to control your body and make it do the thing you want, nothing more and nothing less. How? Practice off stage what you want to perform on stage. We'll talk more about that shortly.

3. Be Comfortable, and You'll Make Your Audience Comfortable

Have you ever watched a training video made by someone who had evidently been told to "talk with their hands," but it was clearly unnatural to them? A robot dance would've been smoother. The video would have been more effective with no gestures at all. That is to say, this chapter may push you to move more than you normally would, but you need to become comfortable by practicing prior to speaking. If you aren't comfortable, your audience will know it. More than that, they'll feel it.

Another way to describe this is "being comfortable in your own skin"—knowing who you are and enjoying being you. This is one of the natural results of doing the work on your identity in Part I. But it's also possible to become *too* comfortable. It might be comfortable for you to walk around your house in your boxers or underclothes, but that's not going to make your guest comfortable. So, if you have guests coming over, you'll put on your comfy jeans and T-shirt. In the same way, you want to be comfortable on stage but still be mindful of how your nonverbals affect your audience. This goes back to the lesson of Chapter 9: It's your job to serve them.

To stretch the clothing analogy a little further, if the setting were more formal than hanging out in your living room, you'd choose nicer clothes but still something that you're comfortable in. Some of your presentations may be casual and others more formal. You want to match your level of comfort and familiarity to that of the audience and the situation.

Whatever the case, your goal is to become comfortable inside yourself—even if the outside requires more decorum. When you're confident in your own skin, the audience feels your confidence and becomes more comfortable in their seats.

When you're confident in your own skin, the audience feels your confidence.

Keeping those principles in the front of your mind, I want to teach you these three nonverbal communication skills: facial expressions, hand gestures, and body movement.

1. FACIAL EXPRESSIONS

Facial expressions are crucial to your communication. They add texture and interest to the spoken word and allow you to connect on a personal level. No matter how stoic you normally are, you need to engage your face while you speak. Expressions are also how you communicate what's actually going on inside. Facial expressions, words, and beliefs must be in alignment. Your audience is extremely perceptive, and if you don't believe what you're saying, they'll see it in your face—and they'll believe your face over your words every time.

Your audience will believe your face over your words every time.

There's a lot going on in your face. Over forty muscles, finely tuned, allow us to show a wide variety of expressions, but most of the action happens around our eyes and mouth. Years ago, I can't remember where, I read that our eyes typically follow a regular pattern when we're in a conversation. We look at the other person's right eye, go to the left, then to the mouth, glance away, and then repeat. Accordingly, we can focus on our eyes and mouth. First, three things about the eyes.

a. Eye Contact

Making eye contact is intimidating to many speakers, so they choose some spot on the wall to focus on. But humans are incredibly attuned to what people are looking at. Your audience may or may not *know* that you aren't looking at them, but they'll *feel* it. And you'll feel the lack of connection as well. Failing to make eye contact with your audience will turn them into a crowd.

I tell my clients, "Don't scan—connect." What I mean is you shouldn't scan the audience like an empty room but connect with people by making brief eye contact with individuals. You're not staring *at* them; you're talking *to* them. Spend a couple of seconds with one person then move to another on the other side of the room. Intentionally make your way around your space.

Don't scan—connect.

What about virtual meetings? I devote a lot of time to this in *Speak & Meet Virtually*, but my most important advice is to treat the camera as if it were the eyes of your audience. Talk into the camera and look into it when listening. You don't have to stare 100% of the time (you wouldn't do that in real life), but focus the majority of your attention there.

One more note on eye contact: I'm speaking primarily to an American audience. Different cultures have different norms. What is polite in one place would be rude in another. In the American business world or a globalized context, follow the American norms of expressing warmth, trust, and confidence through eye contact. But if you're going to travel or interact with another culture, study what is appropriate there.

b. Eyebrows and Surrounding Areas

A lot of emotion is communicated through eyebrows. You might furrow them when you're serious or angry or flit them upward to give your words an ironic flare. The area around our eyes can also communicate if a smile is real or fake. Perhaps you've heard of the Duchenne smile, which is basically a genuine, happy grin. One of its telltale signs is a crinkling of the skin on the outer corner of the eyes, that is, "crow's feet."

c. Eye Shape

By eye shape, I don't mean how they look in a relaxed position, but how we make them bigger or smaller as part of a larger expression. The two most common are wide eyes (expressing surprise, wonder, or a seriousness that causes people to lean in) and narrow eyes (expressing anger, frustration, confusion, or intensity). But the eyes are often undervalued and can express more emotion than we realize.[2]

Mouth

The mouth is clearly central to facial expressions. Smiles, frowns, pouty lips, and the list goes on. I don't need to describe expressions to you because we recognize them intuitively. Two main points, though: First, the mouth is a muscle (a collection of muscles, to be specific), and muscles require stretching and exercise. We'll get to that shortly.

Second, even though expressions are intuitive, we don't always carry that intuition with us on stage. In fact, the pressure to perform can subvert our normal emotional display. This point was made vividly to me when I was taking singing lessons years ago. I was singing a happy song, but the instructor said, "Mike, it looks like you're in agony!" This is more common than you think. I've worked with people who look mad when they're saying something positive, exasperated when they're excited, bored when they're trying to be welcoming. As is often the case, you have to learn how to act naturally. It takes effort to do on stage what you normally do off stage. You have to create awareness of what emotions your face is expressing and connect them with your feelings. Your emotions must match your facial expressions.

Your emotions must match your facial expressions.

AWARENESS AND PRACTICE

To overcome mismatched emotions and facial expressions, start by building awareness. Whether it's "resting bitch face" (a comical description of people who look scornful even when their face is at rest) or letting performance anxiety distort your expressions, you need to know what you look like before you can fix it.

Begin by watching close-up videos of your presentations (virtual meetings are great for this) with the sound off. What do your eyes and face seem to be saying? Do they align with your words? Next, ask others to watch you speak and give their observations.

Simply being aware is one of the most important tools for creating alignment. As soon as my singing instructor told me about my agonized look, I simply stopped doing it. Continue to watch your presentations and ask trusted individuals to do the same for you.

Even if your expressions match your emotions, each of us has room for improvement when it comes to showing emotions. As I said earlier, expressions are achieved through using muscles. Muscles require exercise and stretching to operate at their peak. Here are two ways to practice off stage what you want to do on stage.

First is an exercise called the "lion mask/lemon face." It looks silly, and I hate doing it in front of my clients, but it works. Imagine a lion in a full yawn, stretching his mouth out wider than you thought possible. Don't close your eyes though. Widen them as big as they'll go. Bring the rest of your face into the act—flare your nostrils, push your eyebrows all the way up, even try to stretch your ears out. Hold that expression for a moment, relax, then scrunch your face as tightly as possible, as if you'd just taken a bite out of a lemon—rind and all. Pucker your lips, close your eyes tight, and squeeze your eyebrows in. This is kind of like yoga with your face, going from big, open expressions to small, tight ones, that is, stretch and compress. This exercise strengthens your entire face and acclimates it to a full range of expressions. As with the diction exercises in Chapter 16, use it on a daily basis as well as just before speaking—it's okay to hide out in the bathroom for it.

Second, use the pencil exercise (also in Chapter 16). It not only strengthens your tongue but provides a great opportunity to improve your facial expressions because your face will work in overdrive to overcome the new limitations. Like a blind person with highly attuned hearing, your facial muscles come alive and help you communicate your message through your mouth, eyes, eyebrows, and forehead.

The Mirror Effect

Numerous studies have demonstrated our tendency, as communal beings, to mirror each other's nonverbal communication. Unless you intentionally avoid it, you're prone to match someone's stance, arm position, or facial expression. This means that if you, as the speaker, smile and are open, your audience will typically smile and be open right back (which is a huge confidence builder).

Here's a genius pro tip: Use this to your advantage as a speaker by nodding slightly when you're seeking agreement.

I even caught myself nodding as I worked on this paragraph! It's great for persuading people of any of your ideas or selling them on something.

Be careful, however, because this works in reverse. If an audience appears serious, distant, or hostile, your inclination may be to match them. You must carefully lead them into mirroring you instead of you mirroring them.

2. HAND GESTURES

One study researched hundreds of TED Talks and found a surprising correlation (which, of course, does not *prove* causation): The least popular TED Talks had an average of 272 hand gestures during their allotted 18-minute speech, and the most popular had 465. Causation or not, hand gestures have been proven to help people remember your message, making them a great skill to add to your tool belt. Just make sure they abide by the principles I've already given you. They must match your words, you need to remain in control of them and only use them after you've practiced them enough off stage to be comfortable on stage. Add the following don'ts and do's, and your hand gestures will increase your confidence, authority, and effectiveness.

> **Hand gestures have been proven to help people remember your message.**

Don'ts

Don't point at people. Whether it's done with one finger or multiple, it's almost always going to feel aggressive and/or negative.

Don't make a fist with your hand. It will either make you look tense or aggressive.

Don't put your hands in your pockets (but see the exception below). It closes you off, bunches up your shoulders, and conveys insecurity.

Don't put your hands behind your back. It's an unnatural posture.

Don't hold on to the lectern. It becomes an oversized security blanket.

Don't hold anything in your hand. It draws the audience's attention away from you and onto the object (but see the exceptions below).

Don't fiddle with your hands, especially with odd or purposeless gestures. This includes rubbing your hands together or constantly touching your face. For instance, I used to constantly shake my hands to free them from the cuffs of my long-sleeved shirts.

Our eyes are drawn to movement, so these actions will distract your listeners. And, like the fillers from Chapter 15, they get more distracting the more you do it until they become all the audience notices.

Do's

Do keep your hand inside "the box." The boundaries of this box are roughly outlined by your shoulders (top) and your waist (bottom) and your wrists at a comfortable distance from your body (sides). This box will typically shrink for virtual meetings and expand in larger auditoriums. Gestures made outside the box will typically feel uncomfortable to you and look awkward to the audience, but . . . .

Do go outside the box for intentionally big or exaggerated gestures. When I want to talk about the 154–pound marlin that I caught, I have to extend my arms outside the box because it was literally five feet long (and I have pictures to prove it). Exaggerated gestures can also be used for a comical effect, (which is another reason you should stay in the box unless you're trying to be funny).

Do keep your palms open; make all your gestures with an open hand. This doesn't only *signify* openness but does something in your psyche that *makes* you more open. (When I've mediated interdepartmental conflicts, I've required both parties to have their hands resting on their knees, facing upward and with palms open. They think it's crazy, but it makes everyone more open and less defensive.)

Two Exceptions

There are exceptions to every rule. There are times (for instance) to make a fist or point at someone, but you need to understand the risks and do so for specific reasons. Likewise, there are certain times you should break the "no hands in pockets" and "no items in hands" rules.

As I said, having your hand in your pocket erodes confidence—you in yourself and the audience in you. Why? Because it's essentially an attempt to hide. People do the same thing at parties by "hiding" behind a coffee cup, cigarette, cocktail, or phone. However, I will intentionally put my hand in a pocket—briefly—when I want to shift the atmosphere and make it less formal. So, only put your hand in your pocket if (1) it's intentional, (2) it's brief, and (3) you're confident enough not to need it.

Regarding having a physical object in your hand: Any item you hold will grab attention. For that reason, only hold something if you want people to notice it. One of my favorite tricks for really emphasizing a quote is to write it on a 3×5 card and keep it in my suit jacket. At the right time, I'll pull it out, and all eyes are immediately drawn to it. I may not read it right away but draw in their interest through delay (remember the Interest Pause in Chapter 15?). Once I do read it, I know that I have everyone's full attention. I could have easily memorized the quote or put it in my notes, but the note card increased its power. The same technique can be used with any sort of item you're using for an object lesson, especially something edible. Try holding a chocolate bar and watch everyone eagerly wait to see what happens with it.

Any item you hold will grab attention.

If you have to use a pointer or clicker for your presentation, try to make it as invisible as possible by (1) keeping it discreetly in one hand, (2) not fiddling with it, and (3) practicing picking it up and putting it down until you can do so seamlessly.

AWARENESS AND PRACTICE

Develop your awareness by watching recordings of your speeches and carefully observe:

- How often do you gesture? The most popular TED Talks averaged one gesture per two seconds and the least popular one per four seconds. What's yours?

- Do your gestures match the words you're saying? Do they add to or distract from the content?

- Are you in control of your gestures?

- Do you look comfortable moving your arms, or is it more like a robot dance?

Have a trusted friend make the same observations and discuss if you need to gesture more, less, or just do them better.

If you realize that you're in the habit of fiddling or if it looks like you aren't in control of your body, then practice speaking without using your hands at all. Just leave them by your side and develop enough confidence to stand there without moving. This doesn't mean you can't move in an actual speech, but practicing this will help you gain confidence in your own being (without movement) while regaining control of your hands.

If you need more gestures to better engage your audience, then practice giving speeches in front of a mirror and trying out various gestures.[3] This will feel awkward at first! That's why you need to (say it with me) practice off stage what you want to do on stage.

3. POSTURE AND BODY MOVEMENT

The third physical nonverbal is your body movement, that is, everything we haven't covered already. Again, remember the three principles: Match movement with the words, be in control of your body, and be comfortable in your own skin. Let's spend just another minute on that last one.

I mentioned Dr. Amy Cuddy's TED Talk at the beginning of this chapter, and now I want to encourage you to watch it yourself because she shows how your body language not only communicates your mindset (and hence affects how people view you) but also how it changes mindset. Here's her million-dollar quote:

Our bodies change our minds, our minds can change our behavior, and our behavior can change our outcomes.[4]

Your body language changes your mindset.

The first part of body language and movement is your posture, that is, how you stand and hold yourself. I'm not a chiropractor or medical professional, so I encourage my clients to meet with their chiropractor to get feedback on their posture. I've done that myself and gained some great pointers. I am, however, an expert on communication, and I can tell you that your posture both demonstrates and builds confidence.

Your body affects your mind on a subconscious level.

Now, let's shift to using your body movement for effective nonverbal communication. The following are my don'ts and do's.

Don'ts

Don't shuffle or rock. Shuffling is moving your feet side to side, and rocking is shifting your weight from foot to foot, causing your upper body to rock sideways. Not only is this distracting, but it also conveys nervousness, uncertainty, and the fact that your body is in control. Here's a great way to minimize rocking: Simply move one of your feet backward about ten inches. This makes it much harder to rock side to side. You might start rocking forward and back a little, but that is far less noticeable.

Don't close up your body by hunching your shoulders, folding your arms, putting your hands in your pockets, or dropping your head.

AWARENESS AND PRACTICE

Visit an established chiropractor or physical therapist to evaluate your posture. He or she can probably give you some exercises to practice. You can further develop your awareness by becoming a posture watcher. Discreetly watch people you don't know and observe their posture and how it shapes your perception of them.

Following Dr. Cuddy's research, regularly practice "power posturing," especially prior to a speech or interview—think of it like stretching your confidence. It's kind of like the "lion mask," except for your entire body. Find a private place, and stretch yourself wide open: shoulders back, chest forward, tilt your head up, and place your fists on your hips. By the way, this is also called the "Wonder Woman" pose. Hold it for two minutes, focusing on feeling confident and comfortable as you do so.

This is basically reverse psychosomatics—your body affecting your mind on a subconscious level. Don't believe me? Try it for yourself. Practice power posturing and observe how you feel. Then try doing what we normally do prior to a big interview. Close yourself up in a chair and look down at a phone. You'll see which one increases confidence.

Don't pace. It's distracting and stressful to the audience and gives off a frenetic energy that will bleed into your speech.

Do's

Do keep your body open. Maintain good posture and use a subtle version of the Wonder Woman pose (no hands on hips required). This also opens up your lungs and allows you to take deep belly breaths, which brings more peace, authority, and clarity to your voice.

Do "face out." In live theater, you almost never turn your back to the audience. I've had several clients who turned a full 90 degrees (i.e. shoulders facing forward) whenever they looked at their PowerPoint presentations, effectively closing them off from the audience. Instead, you should use the theater technique of "facing out," which means never turning more than 45 degrees because you understand that everything you do should be on display. At most, glance at the screen over your shoulder while keeping your body forward. Better yet, have a monitor in front of you.

Do move with intention. Rather than pacing around the stage, "block out" your movements (theater speak for "plan"). One of my favorite techniques mentally dedicates different parts of the stage to specific points or themes. So, I might move to Point A for my first point, then to Point B as I transition to the next point, then Point C, and then back to center for the conclusion.

Do find your neutral stance. This is how you stand "at ease"—comfortable and not hiding behind your lectern, notes, clicker, or even hand gestures. You're fully exposed (I also call this "standing naked") yet fully confident in yourself. To find your neutral stance, start by putting your feet shoulder width apart, then move one foot back a bit, and put your weight on that foot. Next, reach your hands straight up to the sky and let them drop. Your hands will fall to their natural place. Roll your shoulders back for better posture. Finally, raise your chin very slightly, look forward, and smile!

AWARENESS AND PRACTICE

Watch some of your speeches (yet again). This time focus on your posture and stance. Evaluate it based on the do's and don'ts above. What areas need the most work?

Practice your neutral stance. Move out of it and back in repeatedly until you can return to neutral out of habit.

DIRECT, NOT DISTRACT

Over the past several chapters, I've given you a full tool belt's worth of skills. I suggest that you actively practice and add to them. But always remember that their purpose is to direct the listener back to your message and never distract from it. That seems obvious, but it's easy to get so caught up in using our skills that we forget their purpose.

Think of it this way. If I were to speak to your organization wearing a really bright fluorescent neon shirt, all you'd think about is how bright my shirt was. Your attention would be distracted from my message. If, however, I wore some regular business casual clothes, you'd give it about one second's thought, thinking, "Okay, that's a respectable person; I can listen to him." After that, you wouldn't think about my clothes again. Mission accomplished.

With every skill you learn and practice, your goal is always for it to be like a perfectly clean window that allows your audience to see straight through to what you're saying. That is the purpose of skills: to help others better understand your message.

CONCLUSION

"Mike, do you really think I can become a better, more
confident speaker? How do I get there? How long
will it take?"

These aren't the exact words that potential clients use, but
they're the sentiment. The answer to the first ones is easy:
"Absolutely, positively, without a doubt, yes!"

You can be a confident speaker. I have never met a hopeless
case, and I never will. But how long will it take? There are three
components that dictate that: your knowledge, your starting
point, and your commitment.

1. Your Knowledge

This book has given you all the knowledge you need. I don't
mean I've written the final word on the topic—there's always
more you can learn. That's the problem. If you wait until you
know everything, you'll never get started. At some point, studying becomes a form of procrastination and a way to avoid change
(because change is hard and scary). I've given you everything you
need to become a confident speaker.

**If you wait until you know everything, you'll
never get started.**

2. Your Starting Point

Not everyone starts at the same place. If someone grew up in a
supportive family that pushed them to succeed and believe in

themselves and was mentored by an experienced speaker, they'll have a head start on someone who grew up in an abusive family. You can't do anything about the advantages or disadvantages you face; all that matters is doing the best with what you've got.

All that matters is doing the best with what you've got.

There's a story that Jesus told of an estate owner that entrusted three servants with different amounts of money, measured in "talents" (that's the source of the English word, by the way), to see how they'd invest it.[1] Five talents were given to one, two to another, and one to the last. The first two servants doubled their money, but the last one buried his talent because he was afraid of failing. Here's an interesting thing about the story a lot of people miss: At the end of the story, the estate owner equally honored both servants who doubled their talents. He cared more about what they did with what they'd been given than the net results.

I want you to objectively gauge where you currently are in each of the three sources of confidence and mark it on a scale of 0 to 10 below. Your answers collectively represent your starting point, which affects how long it will take for you to become a more confident speaker.

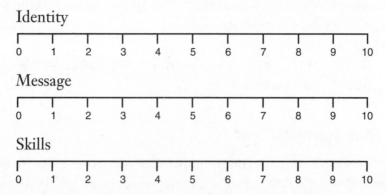

Identity

```
┌───┬───┬───┬───┬───┬───┬───┬───┬───┬───┐
0   1   2   3   4   5   6   7   8   9   10
```

Message

```
┌───┬───┬───┬───┬───┬───┬───┬───┬───┬───┐
0   1   2   3   4   5   6   7   8   9   10
```

Skills

```
┌───┬───┬───┬───┬───┬───┬───┬───┬───┬───┐
0   1   2   3   4   5   6   7   8   9   10
```

If you wanted to run a marathon, your starting point would determine how long it would take to train. If you can already run a half marathon, it would be less time than if a flight of stairs has you sweating profusely. But just because your starting point is farther back, doesn't mean that you can't get there. There are many inspirational stories of ninety-year-old grandmas or disabled individuals conquering great challenges to run marathons. Likewise, a speaker who is extremely nervous, doesn't understand their identity, and has a thick accent can still become a great speaker, but it may take a little longer.

This is key to understand: Your starting point has absolutely no impact on how far you can go. Using the marathon analogy, there is no reason that a former couch potato couldn't outrun the half-marathoner. It all comes down to the third component.

Your starting point has absolutely no impact on how far you can go.

3. Your Commitment

In the movie *Gattaca*, Ethan Hawke's genetically "inferior" character (Vincent) is able to beat genetically engineered characters because of his commitment. He wanted his dream so bad that he did whatever it took to reach it. In a climactic scene, he outswims his "perfected" brother (Anton). Far from shore, Anton shouts, "Vincent! How are you doing this? How have you done any of this? We have to go back!"

"You want to know how I did it?" Vincent says. "This is how I did it, Anton. I never saved anything for the swim back."

You *can* be a confident speaker, leader, and person, fully comfortable in your own skin, able to address a thousand people in an auditorium, or answer the CEO's questions in the boardroom.

How badly do you want it?

What's it worth to you?

I've given you the knowledge. Your starting point is set. The only thing you can do anything about is your commitment. That is your difference maker.

Will it be hard work?

Absolutely. You'll have to push yourself harder—mentally and emotionally—than you thought possible. You can't leave anything for the trip back. But once you're there, confident and unafraid, feeling the joy of giving a great presentation without worrying what anyone thinks of you, you won't ever want to go back.

NOTES

CHAPTER 4

1. Dante, Canto III, trans. by John Ciardi, first edition (New York: W. W. Norton & Company, November 17, 1977).

CHAPTER 5

1. Scott Barry Kaufman, "Unraveling the Mindset of Victimhood," *Scientific American*, June 29, 2020, https://www.scientificamerican.com/article/unraveling-the-mindset-of-victimhood
2. The Gospel of John 5:1–17.
3. Kathryn J. Lively, Affirmations: The Why, What, How, and What If?" *Psychology Today*, March 12, 2014, https://www.psychologytoday.com/us/blog/smart-relationships/201403/affirmations-the-why-what-how-and-what-if

CHAPTER 11

1. *Write to Speak* was written over two years ago, and I've continued refining my system. For that reason, there are differences in how I now describe the system here, but the framework is the same.
2. "John Cleese on Creativity in Management," https:///www.youtube.com/watch?v=Pb5oIIPO62g

CHAPTER 13

1. William Strunk Jr., and E. B. White, *The Elements of Style*, 3rd ed. (New York: Macmillan, 1979).

CHAPTER 14

1. James 1:23–24, author's paraphrase.
2. Abraham Kaplan, *The Conduct of Inquiry: Methodology for Behavioural Science* (Abingdon: Routledge, 1998), p. 28.

CHAPTER 18

1. The most popular one, done by Dr. Mehrabian in the 1960s, cites the figure of 93%, but other researchers have questioned his results.
2. Google "expressive eyes" or see this collection of historical photographs: Lina D, "21 Powerful Photos of People's Eyes That Say More Than Words Ever Could," https://www.boredpanda.com/powerful-photos-of-peoples-eyes
3. This video offers some great suggestions: "What to Do with Your Hands while Speaking? Effective Hand Gestures for Tour Guides," https://www.youtube.com/watch?v=4PMy1dJ1hDo
4. Amy Cuddy, "Your Body Language May Shape Who You Are," https://www.ted.com/talks/amy_cuddy_your_body_language_may_shape_who_you_are

CONCLUSION

1. Matthew 25:14-30.

ABOUT THE AUTHOR

Mike Acker is a keynote speaker, author, and executive communication coach with over twenty years of speaking, leadership development, and organizational management experience.

Beyond corporate training, Mike engages in his community as a Seattle TEDx speaker coach and works with international agencies to provide relief amidst poverty.

Mike also enjoys rock-climbing, wake surfing, skiing, church, building Legos with his son, Paxton, and going on dates with his wife, Taylor. Mike believes in the power of prayer, exercise, journaling, and real community to counter the stresses of everyday life.

http://www.mikeacker.com

Explore The Public Speaking School and work personally with Mike Acker:

| **1-on-1 Coaching** | **Professional Online Course Curriculum** | **Monthly Mastermind Cohort** |

Create Confidence through Communication.

1. Overcome insecurity and anxiety.
2. Learn how to connect with others.
3. Develop Executive Presence.

Don't wait: set up a free consultation:
https://advance.as.me/SWNF

(Available for individuals and teams)

BOOK MIKE ACKER

FOR YOUR TEAM OR EVENT

Mike Acker is an in-demand keynote speaker on effective communication, emotional intelligence, and transformational leadership. His work in coaching, writing, and speaking inspires audiences around the nation and the globe. His first book, *Speak with No Fear*, achieved the status of the highest-ranking book on overcoming nervousness in speaking.

He has worked with Adobe, Amazon, Microsoft, Oracle, INOApps, Dallas International School, U.S. federal agencies, the International Monetary Fund, and many others.

If you are interested in booking Mike Acker for a keynote presentation, workshop, or virtual program, please contact info@mikeacker.com or visit www.MikeAcker.com.

Past Engagements Include:

INDEX

Voice clarity, 175–187
  barriers to, 179–185
  changing one's voice, 175–177
  understanding of others, 177–179
Von Trapp, Maria, 117

W
Walk the Line (film), 102
Washington State, 33
Weaknesses, *see* strengths and
        weaknesses
Wealth, xiii

Wilson, Russell, 74
Wilson, Woodrow, 110
Word emphasis exercises, 198
Work, current, 50–51
Write to Speak (Acker), 115

Y
You, as message, 13–21

Z
Z factor, 197–198
Zoom meetings, 105